PURE BALANCE

Your Simple Guide to Self-Healing, Growth, and Empowerment for Optimal Health and Well-Being

Clare Evans

BALBOA.
PRESS

A DIVISION OF HAY HOUSE

Balboa Press books may be ordered through booksellers or by contacting:

Balboa Press
A Division of Hay House
1663 Liberty Drive
Bloomington, IN 47403
www.balboapress.com.au
1 (877) 407-4847

Because of the dynamic nature of the Internet, any web addresses or
links contained in this book may have changed since publication and
may no longer be valid. The views expressed in this work are solely those
of the author and do not necessarily reflect the views of the publisher,
and the publisher hereby disclaims any responsibility for them.

The author of this book does not dispense medical advice or prescribe
the use of any technique as a form of treatment for physical, emotional,
or medical problems without the advice of a physician, either directly
or indirectly. The intent of the author is only to offer information
of a general nature to help you in your quest for emotional and
spiritual wellbeing. In the event you use any of the information in
this book for yourself, which is your constitutional right, the author
and the publisher assume no responsibility for your actions.

Any people depicted in stock imagery provided by Thinkstock are
models, and such images are being used for illustrative purposes only.
Certain stock imagery © Thinkstock.

Print information available on the last page.

ISBN: 978-1-4525-2960-8 (sc)
ISBN: 978-1-4525-2961-5 (e)

Balboa Press rev. date: 08/06/2015

Pure; clean and free from impurities; sheer or complete; clear and vivid.

Balance; a state of equilibrium or equipoise; equality in amount, weight, value, or importance.

Dedicated to my loving husband Peter and

beautiful daughters Paige and Amber,

with so much love.

Thank you for your unconditional love and support

along every step of my journey, and

being everything I ever wished for! xx

CONTENTS

FOREWORD

It is with joy I introduce you to this delightful companion. Clare's heart and soul can be found sprinkled lightly through the words, images, and actions. Don't be misled, no creative work just appears—the struggle, determination, and sheer hard work must be acknowledged. So as you delve deeper the enormous sense of the wonder of the *Universe* emerges.

Clare steps you into awareness and allows you the tools that access your true self. She lovingly shares ways for you to invite within everything needed to be your best *you*!

This is a world that needs as much love, joy, and imagination as we have to share. This simple self-first guide will make an impact on what you do today; how you carry it into tomorrow, and what opens up in your Universe. Enjoy the wellness, wonder, and warmth.

Christine Bottrell, Ph D.

PREFACE

If you'd of asked me about ten years ago where I'd be in ten years time, I would have never thought that I'd go through what I have, or be who and where I am today. I have been on the most amazing personal journey with absolute highs, lows, and everything in between!

In early 2007, I appeared to have everything I'd ever dreamed of; husband, children, job, house, family, and friends. I wasn't fully aware of it at the time, but it was a different story on the inside. I hated my body, worried about everything, and took on other people's problems. I gave away my power, attempted to be a perfectionist, and drank way too much alcohol for my small body too. I was so hard on myself, emotionally over-sensitive, and was "in the closet" spiritually—and out of touch with it. I ate what I thought was a healthy diet and I also exercised a lot—fortunately, as this helped me to identify when something was very wrong.

It was no doubt the major turning point in my life when I was diagnosed with cancer in late 2007, right about the time of my thirtieth birthday. With a young family my world was turned upside down. Yet after the initial shock I actually faced my mortality and completely surrendered to it. In faith I said to the angels and the Divine, "If it's my time to go, I'll go... however, if I have a choice—I choose to stay!" I knew my life would never be the same again.

As well as accepting modern medicine's intensive chemotherapy treatment, I did everything I possibly could to get to remission in the quickest probable time. I drank fresh vegetable and fruit juices every day and did gentle exercise. I left my place of employment and started painting again, avoided un-well people, and allowed others to take care of me. I went back to meditation group too—reconnecting with my spirituality. I continued the same "healthy" diet as before... plus chocolate, of course!

During my sixth and final round of chemotherapy I'd had enough, and my body was telling me so. It was the only time I experienced extreme nausea during the actual administration of those toxic drugs. I simply *knew* the cancer was gone from my body.

Following remission I got back into life—perhaps a little too much at times. I hit the champagne hard and pushed myself physically through running. Emotionally I became a wreck and soon developed depression and bulimia. There were times that I was more aligned with the real me though. I loved meditating and all things spiritual yet still kept much of that to myself, for fear of judgement by others. Life for me was up and down like a yo-yo. Then I thought to myself, "Hang on a minute Clare, if I can get through cancer I can get through any obstacle and, I can *do* anything!"

I began to detox; mentally, physically, emotionally, and spiritually, releasing the layers I'd been carrying. I allowed others to assist me in healing and cut out a lot of rubbish to consume a healthier diet. I went on retreats and made a career change from administration to reflexology, and loved my new work! Now I was really beginning to heal.

I became so inspired as I embarked on an intense journey of self-discovery, healing, growth, and empowerment. I was on a one way mission to become the healthiest and happiest version of myself. I read more self-help books, moved across to the other side of the country with my family, studied holistic counselling—and a lot of the counselling was done on myself! I began to love and nurture myself, meditated, journalled, and spent more time in nature. I also re-framed my thoughts and beliefs, embraced my power, and began to express my *true* self. I was really letting go and flowing as I'd changed and improved on many things in my life—both within and without. Most notably was my gradual dietary change that was originally a standard Australian diet (SAD), to eventually consuming a nutritious plant-based diet. Yes, the majority of what I eat now is vegetables and fruit, and I'm *loving* it!

In 2013, after five years in remission, I was officially termed "*cured*". That filled me with joy and inspiration! I felt happier, healthier, balanced, and more than ever before the most authentic version of myself. I enjoyed the fact that I had really begun to live an intuitive, healthy, and balanced lifestyle.

I began to fill my days as an aspiring health and wellbeing coach, speaker, and writer. It's been a true blessing to have assisted and been witness to (the varying stages of) healing, growth, and empowerment of others throughout the years of conducting my own private practice. However, my business and I had many ups and downs.

CLARE EVANS

There were times when I simply knew I was following my destiny, yet others when the world around me just didn't seem to reflect that personal faith. I struggled to understand why the Universe didn't seem to support me and why things weren't happening sooner, when I was supposedly following my guidance and working so hard. A publishing agreement turned out to be more of a scam than a forward step in my career as an author, at the same time as losing a young friend to cancer. Soon after that was when I became totally miserable and majorly depressed. So much so that at this time, I actually wanted out of this life!

Of course much of this was a private pain and consulting a doctor was the only logical thing I could think to do next. I needed some Western medical intervention as I believed I'd been doing all I could holistically and knew the signs of depression—I'd been there before. I soon met with my next huge life challenge and the healing journey continued. Not only was I majorly depressed, but it was suggested I may have bipolar disorder.

Once again my world was turned upside down and inside out! *"I can't have bipolar, I'm a healer! How can I possibly work with people when I'm struggling with a "mood disorder" myself? How could this even happen, when my self-care and holistic lifestyle is so good? I do everything I can possibly think of to be in full health!"*

I threw a huge internal tantrum and soon took time off from working with others, to focus on my own healing once more. This time there was a big focus on going deeper, much deeper to address my lack of ease (dis-ease). I gained a lot of first hand mental-health experience and understanding, especially through the assistance of an amazing holistic counsellor. We worked specifically on the emotional and mental levels, right to the core (beliefs) and ultimate cause—that had been locked away in my subconscious mind for thirty-five years! This combined with a few more lifestyle changes and taking my spiritual connections to a new level, meant that I was able to begin to manage my condition fairly well.

In 2014, at 10am on the 10th of the 10th—world mental health day, my lovely new psychiatrist confirmed my GP's suggestion and diagnosed me with bipolar disorder II. After three months of the idea I had already accepted it and was ready to move on with my life. All was occurring in divine time. Just as it always has, always does and always will. It wasn't long before the reasoning for my fate became crystal clear to me—as was with the cancer experience—through this I will learn, and what I learn I will then share with others!

Writing was a part of my healing journey and I'd wondered for quite a while why I had been stuck on writing the *mind* chapter of this book. That was because first I had to learn about it through experiencing it directly myself, and to go through further healing. When I did I began to align my conscious and subconscious mind. What followed was a profoundly deep spiritual connection, and a renewed passion and inspiration to write. The final piece of the puzzle was soon in place and then finally after more than five years, it all came together—to be the book that you are holding in your hands this very moment.

As you may gather I am truly passionate about spirit, energy, and love, as well as healing, personal growth, and empowering others. This, along with my intuition leads me in everything I do, and flows into every area of my life—especially my work.

Perhaps you don't have the awareness that holistic healing modalities exist, or are isolated and therefore, not able to visit practitioners like myself in person. Possibly you haven't yet seen the immense value in investing in your own self-care. This is where my new baby (this book) comes in. I wish to provide a valuable and affordable resource so that *everyone* may have the opportunity to begin or continue their journey, and gain self-awareness towards balance and optimal wellbeing.

The decline in health and wellbeing of the global population is an ongoing and growing issue in the world today, over burdening health systems. Rather than focussing on and accepting a "band aid approach" for a cure, *Pure Balance* aims at shifting your perspective towards self, positive change, and preventative health through action. The amazing technology of modern medicine combined with complementary therapies thousands of years old allows a holistic approach to health and wellbeing. This is where people can often heal the symptom, the ailment, and the underlying cause of their dis-ease.

Just as every system in our physical bodies effects all others, so too do the different aspects of our personal selves. As an example, if you haven't done any physical activity for a few days you may start to emotionally feel down. This highlights the effects of one area of imbalance and the importance of (whole) balance, adding to our ease.

Through the powerfully simplistic words of this book I lead you through the study I've undertaken, my experiences of working with clients, and my own personal journey. Mentally I have challenged and changed beliefs, and learnt to respond rather than react, as well as the power of perception—that allows me to live more consciously. Physical changes include; vastly improving my diet—focussing on nutrition, regulating sleep patterns, and committing to daily activity. Emotionally I now acknowledge and release stored emotions. I have healed relationships and also recognise and live daily through emotional intelligence. Spiritually I have discovered my authentic and true self and now share my voice—that allows me to become empowered in love, my spirit shining through the surface. Those around me now know who I really am.

This has been quite enlightening, however, the keystone was when I learnt to be fully aware of keeping the balance as best I could of *all* of these areas. Balance of mind, body, heart, and spirit allows one to feel their best, centred, empowered, and ultimately set up to enjoy a happy and fulfilled life on earth. I want that for you too!

My hope is that you can relate to my messages and see that transformation of your being is totally do-able (not above and beyond that it only looks dreamy). Many dreamers may not make the choice and take action to achieve those dreams, particularly through hard work and challenging times. I believe it's different for you because you've picked up this book.

Thank you for choosing to act now towards finding personal balance through reading *Pure Balance*. It was written "in love" by me for you, and serves as a simple tool to support and guide you towards optimal health and wellbeing. I truly hope my words and actions will gently inspire you to create permanent positive change and improvements within yourself, and your life!

Throughout you'll find the inclusion of various activities and exercises. To enhance the healing experience I suggest you purchase yourself a beautiful new personal journal specifically for their completion. Journaling also aids as a tool for self-reflection and expression, as well as monitoring the progress of your health and wellbeing journey.

I invite you to let go of the focus on the outside world as you read through the following pages. Please choose a time that you will not be disturbed, to allow yourself to be aware of and connect exclusively with yourself. (Not the kids, the few dishes that might be still in the sink or what you should've done differently yesterday. Not what you have to do today, or next week... or next year either!) The natural nurturers of the world, commonly known as "givers" or "peacemakers", often put the needs of others before their own only to find their own needs neglected. I know from firsthand experience.

So please begin the exciting journey by giving yourself the love and attention you deserve. This is vital self-care so you may truthfully receive and accept the internal answers to questions like, "where am I currently at?" and "who and where do I actually want to be?" The benefits go way beyond self as you begin to find your balance, shine, and infuse our planet with your positive energy.

Happy reading!

With much love and blessings to you,
Clare xx

ACKNOWLEDGEMENTS

There are many people to thank as I am truly grateful for every person who's been a part of my amazing life to date.

First off; to my soul mate, life partner, best friend, and loving husband, Pete. How blessed were we to have found each other so very young and yet not let anything deter us from our destined life together. You have been what many would call my "rock", right beside me through so many personal challenges. Yet with unwavering dedication to our relationship and faith in me we have not only shared our lives, but healed, grown, and continue to blossom together, in love. Thank you for your eternal love, believing in me, and supporting me wholeheartedly—especially with my work and vision.

Secondly my two very gorgeous daughters, Paige and Amber! Thank you for choosing me to be your mother this lifetime. I'm grateful for the challenges, total love, joy moments, and everything in between. Such little teachers you are! xx

Beautiful Mumma Delys and Pappa Guy—for the absolute love and support that you have provided my entire life, I thank you so much. You've been there every step of the way seeing the good, the bad, and the ugly through my personal transformation. Now the rose is in full bloom.

The soul sista connections—you know who you are—I have so much love for you beautiful ladies.

To all my other immediate and extended family and friends; thank you for accepting me for who I am and for what you have taught me over the years.

It is with gratitude that I acknowledge my earthly spiritual teachers, particularly; Gerry, Gladys, Jenice, and Sharon. Thank you for your love and support in assisting me to be my own greatest teacher!

As well as those mentioned above, the following have also assisted me greatly along my healing and growth journey; Dr Carl Staer, Dr Kris Barrett, and Dr Rosie Saxton; Brigitte, Cindy, Elizabeth, Kate, Mat, Robyn, Stephanie, Sue, and Vicki—thank you all so very much.

Thank you to the following who have been highly influential authors, teachers and mentors to me, at various times; Dr Brian L. Weiss, Dr Joel Fuhrman, Dr Wayne W. Dyer, Doreen Virtue, James Van Praagh, Kris Carr, Lisa Williams, Louise L. Hay, Reid Tracy, and Sonia Choquette.

Pete and Christine, thank you for your honest comments, bold suggestions, and exceptional editorial assistance. Your aid and support of "my baby" means so much to me.

A big thank you goes to all the wonderful souls at the Balboa Press division of Hay House who were involved in the process of publishing this book. Together we made my dream of becoming a published author a reality!

My reflexology, meditation, holistic counselling, energy healing and coaching clients who allowed me to personally assist them along their journey, you have also greatly assisted me! Through "practice" I fine-tuned how I personally perceive and work with energy. Over the years I grew to trust in what I received from spirit, giving me confidence to pass along the necessary information to you, so I thank you!

To all others who have ever crossed my path, thank you for the experiences and giving me some of the lessons I've needed to learn.

Finally and very importantly to you, the reader! This book had been a clear vision for quite some time and now it's a reality. Perhaps one day we too will personally cross paths. Thank you for choosing this book and allowing me to be of assistance to you along your journey.

May you be the absolute best version of yourself, live a life of balance, and shine your light and love. Together we can make this world a beautiful, harmonious, and peaceful place for us all to live.

My love goes out to you all, now and forever... xx

CHAPTER 1

DEVELOPING BALANCE

Balance occurs on all levels of our being: mind, body, heart, and spirit. When we are really in balance, we feel whole and complete. We are happy, healthy, and confident. We are a joyful and loving person, with a positive outlook on life. Every moment of every day is embraced, and we are truly living! However, living in the Western world at this point in history makes many of us struggle to understand what it's really like to be in a state of balance.

It could be likened to a chair, generally balanced on all four legs. However, if even just one of those legs is shortened, removed, or falls off, it is impossible for the seat of that chair to be evenly balanced. We would have an uncomfortable time sitting on it, if we could at all. So it is true with us. If we are fairly optimistic in our mind and happy in our heart and spirit, but we have an unhealthy body, then there's no balance. Or if we have a fit body and mind, but we feel little happiness in our hearts or joy in life, there's no balance. Likewise, if we are healthy in body, heart, and spirit, but we think negatively, then there's no balance there either.

Mind, body, heart, and spirit all individually affect each other, just as one system of the human body directly or indirectly affects all of the other systems. For example, if someone who is generally well receives some hurtful comments and takes it to heart, he or she may start feeling lonely and down in spirit. This may begin to affect their body through altering their appetite, perhaps leading to excessive emotional eating. This person may start to put on weight over time, and if that balance is not corrected then it may affect his or her mind by creating negative thoughts about themself and low self-esteem. The downward spiral has commenced, and that person would start to feel very unbalanced indeed. In regards to this example, the person could be heading for a depressed state.

The good news is that no matter what point we are at on a downward spiral—even if at "rock bottom"—we each have the capability to make choices to stop and instigate change, turning things around completely. Thus we begin to heal and move onwards and upwards along the spiral.

Being fully balanced (that I also affectionately refer to as being *in the zone*) however, goes much deeper and is quite multidimensional. What I mean by this is that everyone has had a different experience in life and each is at a different stage and maturity. Regardless of age, some have managed to travel fairly lightly with minimal "layers" built up, that may look a little like this:

~ MINIMAL LAYERS ~

Others may be a little more built up, looking more like these moderate layers:

- MODERATE LAYERS -

And some are weighed down with multiple layers, carrying the most; their true selves are often buried deep inside, making them barely visible under the heavy layers:

- HEAVY LAYERS -

So what are these layers made up of? Basically, they are a sum of our past experiences that we are still choosing to carry—whether we are aware of it or not. They include our burdens, irrational beliefs, hurts, and guilts. It also includes our fears, anxieties, worries, and self-doubts. This is along with any angers, resentments, frustrations, and hates too. Sound heavy? It is not only heavy, but it is often toxic as well. These layers might be of mental, emotional, physical, or spiritual origin and can be deposited in any of these areas of our being, with varying density.

Some layers may be heavy and dark, while some are thinner and lighter. And the more layers there are, the longer and more in-depth the healing is likely to be. In saying that though, some individuals have a determined focus and are prepared to do whatever is necessary. This subsequently enables them to heal at a rather rapid rate! As human beings our ability to self-heal is truly amazing, and each person is in fact their own healer. Yes, no one can heal us—we can only heal ourselves.

Fortunately we are able to release these layers and begin with an awareness of what our layers are. Through releasing them we make room for the assimilation of new, positive, and empowering aspects. You may prefer to but you don't need to go it alone. There are many lovely people in the world who are ready and willing to assist you.

Traditional Western medicine and health care is generally the first port of call, and at times it needs to be sought. However, I'm referring to complementary medicine that is highly beneficial in healing some issues, not limited to the physical body. In order to receive comprehensive healing, a combination of both Eastern and Western medical assessment and treatment is required.

Only we can make the decision to heal ourselves, but we may need some of those lovely others along the way. You may find assistance through a trusted friend or relative, or you may prefer to seek the confidential and professional assistance of a qualified complementary-health therapist or practitioner. When working with "healers", please remember that they don't actually heal you, as their title suggests. They merely hold the energetic space at as high and fine a level as possible for them, and they provide the tools that you can utilise to instigate your own change. You hold the power and ability to change your life in the most remarkable of ways. You get to choose to be who you really are and create the life that you aspire to live because *you are your own healer!* I'm not sure about how you feel, but I feel full of excitement for you at the possibilities!

Sometimes healing can feel like you are taking two steps forward and one step back. What's important is to keep facing forward! It is said that it takes twenty-one days to change a habit, and small gradual changes will be the most sustainable. It's one step at a time. Then, once those changes have been implemented, more positive changes can be made.

If you get to the unfortunate point of heavy layers, then in order for you to get out of the "black hole," you need to reverse the spiralling and begin your journey back to a balanced state. This takes unwavering commitment and perseverance to achieve optimal results! Obviously the greater the imbalance, the greater the challenge will be moving back to wholeness. But it can and absolutely will happen—if you choose.

At this very moment in your life, you are presented here with a wonderful opportunity for personal change—that could be seen as a crossroads or "sliding doors" moment for you. The question is; are you comfortable and/or set in your ways? Or, are you prepared and able to step up and outside your comfort zone, to take a chance, to see yourself in truth, and to change yourself and your life—for the better? If you are comfortable, you may let this opportunity pass and everything will stay the same as before—and that is perfectly natural and acceptable! However, if you choose to take a leap of faith—and particularly if your heart sings out *yes!*—then you will not only begin an exciting new chapter of your life, but you will potentially change your entire world in profound and amazing ways! People go through rapid personal growth and do incredible things when prepared to let go of the old and invest in themselves, in their health and in their wellbeing.

You may already know some people who are living happy, healthy lives, highlighting the benefits of living a life of wellbeing. The more you pay attention to others leading by example, the more inspired you become to make positive changes. This ultimately leads to the enhancement of your own wellbeing. You then will likely prompt the healing in others as you to begin to lead by example too.

It is fantastic to see some health-care practitioners in the Western world opening up to and incorporating Eastern philosophies as part of their routine; combining Western medicine with complementary therapies and not merely prescribing a pill for most ailments. This provides much needed holistic healing for patients. Modern medicine is amazing, especially for diagnosing disease in the earliest of stages through medical imaging. With openness to a combination of the two approaches, patients have the ability heal at a more productive and efficient pace. While there are an extraordinary number of cancer types, the layers of life and experience must be taken into account. Treatment through chemotherapy and radiation is only a part of the healing. I witnessed a couple of other people who experienced the same type of cancer as me around the same time as I did. A few years on, I remained in remission; however, one relapsed and the other sadly passed away.

While we are all on our individual journeys, this is when I realised that for complete healing patients must be assisted to heal their *whole being*. While intensive treatment may be the main priority and life-saving at first, a focus on the mental, emotional, spiritual, and social factors (along with diet and exercise) must be included. This is complementary therapy, and there are some brilliant cancer-care centres operating now right across the globe. They provide an efficient and holistic nature of care. For that we can all be grateful.

Can everyone heal? Unfortunately, there are times when people don't heal, regardless of all that is done for their healing. The first is when it's their time to leave this earth in the physical form—it's their time to die. The focus then moves to loving care and making them as comfortable and peaceful as possible in pleasant surrounds. That will provide them with the required nurturing environment for their transition to the after-life world of spirit. The second exception to those who don't heal are those who are capable (they aren't going anywhere!) but don't actually choose to take required action. These people may feel that they don't have the strength—that they just can't do it, or perhaps they aren't yet ready to face the truth.

I completely understand that your own truth can be confronting and daunting, yet the intention of healing is to release what no longer serves you and assimilate what does. Real healing causes no further harm, allows you to find your balance, and your true self emerges. You are the only one responsible for holding onto your layers. The layers may be a combination of traumatic experiences, limited beliefs, unhealthy habits, and repressed emotions. You may not even know you are carrying them! *You* are responsible for releasing what no longer serves you, and for building a refreshed version of yourself (and consequently a refreshed life). Step by step you make your way towards self-fulfilment, peace, contentment, empowerment, health, and wellbeing.

In the upcoming pages I'll provide you with an opportunity to shift that responsibility into choice and action, by working through various reflection and journaling exercises.

Self-Awareness

You are totally unique and truly amazing!

I think that line calls to be repeated...

You are totally *unique* and truly *amazing!*... and it's as simple as that.

Do you actually comprehend how awesome you are? It's true! Connect with that concept for just a moment... as you affirm it to yourself; *"I am unique and amazing!"*

The intention is not to pump up your ego here, but to appeal to your higher self to step forward!

Every person was born into this world with their very own set of skills and qualities—attributes that makes them like no other. No two people are exactly the same, yet (at the risk of sounding contradictory) by an invisible force we are all connected, as one. At the centre of each and every human being is the essence of pure divine love—essentially a little piece of the Divine (God). You might think of it as the diamond within. However, with varying conditions—environment, circumstances, challenges, lifestyle, beliefs, and habits, we can develop these layers over time. These layers influence us and create our own ever changing personal energy. By adulthood that essence of pure divine love may well be buried deep, perhaps very deep in some. It may still occasionally shine to the surface, with a glimmer of light. Everyone, no matter what we have been through, has the capability of healing, growing, and becoming self-empowered... if only we so choose. Then we must commit to follow up that choice with the necessary action. This is not to be viewed as a "once off" healing, where things go back to how they were prior. True healing instigates such deep changes and improvements in order to "find your true self". You must understand that once you begin the journey, your life will never be the same again. It will very likely be *so much better* than before! (Woo hoo!)

Every person was born a vibrational being, emitting a scientifically proven electro-magnetic field (our personal energy). Some "energy sensitive" people (whether they consciously know it or not) are even able to "read" that energy. More and more people are becoming aware, opening up to sensing energy, and learning to "trust their vibes"—both their own and what they pick up from others.

Your personal energy is a reflection of the combination of all you are in any given moment. For example, if we are attached to others this will be reflected, as will lack of self-esteem and confidence. I will expand on this further in upcoming chapters. Through self-focus you are actually able to perceive your own personal energy, and with the aid of some effective tools, make the necessary adjustments. Your personal energy will begin to reflect your personal integrity, as your higher self steps forward.

A balanced life is built from the inside out, and thus we must tune out the external influences for a moment and return to self. This is basically a form of meditation or self-reflection. Many people often spend so much time looking outside of themselves... looking for all the answers. However, in reality *the answers lie within*. Personal wisdom is a combination of knowledge and experience. Each one of us holds that special key to unlock our own inner wisdom to achieve our infinite potential...

There's no better time like the present to turn the key. There is no point living in the past, it's done. It's time to let it go. There's no point living in the future either... for who knows what tomorrow will bring?! As Louise L. Hay states in her book *Heal Your Body*, "*The point of power is in the present moment*". By living in the now, we can also get very creative and manifest the life of our dreams; for today's thoughts, words, and actions pave the pathway for tomorrow's amazing experiences...

It is because you are "one of a kind" that your own healing, growth, and empowerment experience towards balance, will also be unique to you. What you need will be different to what someone else needs. What works for someone else may not work for you. Likewise, what works for you may not work for someone else. It is up to you to discover what you need, and take action if you choose to instigate changes to improve your life. Just as no other person can digest the food we eat for us, no one else can live our lives either. Individuals are often far more influenced by others than what many realise. Again, the first step to living a life of balance is to retreat and take some quiet time on your own to reconnect with your true self. This is not selfish, but self-first and absolutely necessary if you are to become the most authentic version of you.

Cell biologist Bruce H. Lipton, Ph D, believes most people operate from their subconscious minds, most of the time. According to Dr. Lipton in his book *The Biology of Belief* our subconscious mind is "programmed" by our environment—including people around us, up to the age of six. Our habits and beliefs are developed on this experience. Effectively one would be operating from the subconscious (on auto-pilot) and this is why many consider their genes the reason behind who they are and how they behave. Ancestral patterns are effectively passed down from generation to generation. We do as we learn, just as those before us did. Unaware individuals are effectively operating mostly from their subconscious, on auto-pilot.

Awareness is the ability to stop and step back from the conditioning of our upbringing, in order to begin viewing from the conscious perspective of our higher selves and seeing the whole picture. We can then choose to re-program our beliefs, create new habits, and become more balanced. We effectively change ancestral patterns and shift to operate less from the subconscious and more from the conscious mind of our higher selves.

You may have really lost connection with who you truly are and are concreted in your conditioned ways, operating from the subconscious mind. Let's face it, change can be down-right scary, but in truth things are always changing and revolving. Just take a look at nature, and in particular the seasons. On this journey of awakening, if you encounter any resistance allow the thoughts and feelings to surface, then choose to let them go. Through awareness turn resistance into acceptance, and shift your focus to your choice of moving towards optimal health and wellbeing. There is a saying that goes, "feel the fear and do it anyway"... plus, by releasing these fear based emotions you will have more clarity to move forward, towards the direction of balance, and as you go along it will become easier. You may even begin to anticipate change and welcome it with open arms. Please remember also; we aren't striving towards perfection, just the *best* version of ourselves!

Your life doesn't need to be at a point of total imbalance before you choose to reassess yourself and your life either. You hold the power and are free to choose. You have the choice to enhance yourself and your life, in every moment. Ultimately, *you* create the life you choose to live, through the choices you make and the action you take. Yet unfortunately, quite often it is only when people develop major dis-eases such as cancer, suffer a heart attack or fall into a deep depression before any serious life changes are considered. This is because then, if we want to live, it can't be avoided.

A lot of people living in the world today genuinely think they are in good health and wellbeing, and many are. Countless more are not though, and scores of people expect to continue unhealthy lifestyles, and for their doctor to magically "fix" them with a pill whenever they get sick. Unwell and unbalanced people often turn the attention and power over to someone else without so much as even a thought about self-care or personal development. Their level of awareness does not allow them to recognise the need, or perhaps they are not prepared to look too deeply within and take responsibility for their own health and wellbeing. These people often fall into victimhood, and through lack of self-help are reinforcing their own state of being *and* the need to be rescued by others. Sure these people are alive… but can they really say that they are living a healthy life of balance?!

A life of balance usually requires healthy connections with others. However, when we are with others we are often enmeshed in each other's energy. Before we can balance into the energy of others we need to become familiar with our own personal self and energy. Therefore, the following activities require you to spend some time alone. Think about where you feel happiest; it could be outdoors in nature or a particular corner or space inside your home. You may like to play some gentle music in a naturally lit room.

You don't have to answer all of the questions below in one sitting, and you may like to continue reading the following chapters. You can then come back to answer these questions when it feels right for you. When that time comes take your time when answering, so you may process the information internally and assimilate it fully as you make any necessary adjustments within yourself. Let go and enjoy the process too! If you have already begun your self-discovery and healing journey, I would recommend you review your internal world once again and re-assess. This way you can become aware of any fine-tuning required or to highlight any blockages, new or old.

Self-Reflection Activities

Self-reflection is conducted with a desire to be completely self-honest. Express your truth—first to yourself, and then the world. Choose to value this higher than the possible response of any other person. (Never mind what others think).

The only one to impress at this time is yourself, so please be completely open and receptive to the truth. Allow yourself to sit quietly for a moment and turn your attention inwards.

Leave the outer world behind as you take a few slow deep even breaths, and feel your body become more relaxed. Then with full personal integrity at this time in your life ask yourself;

> **Who am I?**
>
> What traits and roles make up you?
>
> **What qualities do I represent right now?**
>
> **What do I love?**

What do I like to do, that fills my heart with love and joy?

Am I optimistic with an open heart, quite happy with myself and my life?

Or, do I find myself with negative thoughts, and sometimes feel like closing off from the world (or perhaps even that life just isn't really worth living?)

Get right to the depths...

What are my honest current thoughts, emotions, and fears?

What are my weaknesses and strengths?

Is there anything holding me back?

Get to know the real you then ask yourself;

What would I like to change or improve on with my qualities and attitude towards life?

What would I like to bring into my life?

Therefore, what do I need to let go of that is;

- not my own?

- what I no longer need?

- not for my highest good?

Now that you have really considered...

What are my dreams and wishes?

(Dream big!)

What do I really need right now?

Don't worry if your answers seem silly or unrealistic. The point is that they are current, specific, and truthful—from your soul!

If any other questions come to mind answer them too!

Commit to regular self-reflection and journaling—every day if possible—as you explore your internal world with more and more awareness. Express your thoughts and emotions openly and enjoy getting to know yourself more intimately—as you would a new friend who you feel a strong connection with. Continue until you feel you know yourself thoroughly and are in touch with your true essence. You'll find that you begin to enjoy this special time of self-connection and trust in yourself strengthens. You start to love and accept yourself whole heartedly, just the way you are, and can express yourself freely—at least to yourself, in the beginning.

* * * * * * * *

As you begin to express yourself freely, there are various ways your energy is altered through "reframing" thoughts and beliefs:

- · change negative into positive.
- · shift from victimhood to empowerment.
- · convert no choice into having a choice.
- · modify old beliefs into a new changed perception.

Reframing Thoughts and Beliefs Activity

Here we will explore your present thoughts and beliefs about self, family and career/work. Also we look at health, spirituality, life, and perhaps other areas of your life.

Self

I think that I...

I believe that I...

Family

I think that my family...

I believe that my family...

Career/work

I think that my career/work...

I believe that my career/work...

Health

I think that my health...

I believe that my health...

Spirituality

I think my spirituality...

I believe my spirituality...

> **Life**
>
> I think life...
>
> I believe life...

> **Another area of your life:**
>
> I think...
>
> I believe...

Now re-read what you have written, and ascertain whether or not you could reframe your statements to be more optimistic and loving. By reframing any negative, lower vibratory words and phrases, we alter our energy with a new perception.

Our thoughts become our words, that become our expressions, that manifests into our reality... therefore, "catch" any negative thoughts and reframe them to positive, there and then... until your new thoughts become your new reality—more aligned with your true self!

* * * * * * * *

Through self-awareness and positive change, we create a favourable shift and alteration of our personal energy. We begin to learn and grow in concurrence with finding our balance. These modifications occur from being fully present.

The Now

Many people new to this way of being require constant cues as a reminder that *the point of power is in the present moment*. At various times in our lives we may find ourselves in the past, or in the future, yet where we really are is in the present! Here we will explore the past, present, and future a little deeper, with the intention of highlighting the need for us all to be and live fully, in present time.

First we will look at the *past*.

You are a sum of all your beliefs, thoughts, words, actions, attitudes, and experiences up to this point and what's done is done. There is simply no turning back the clock and changing things. Even if you could, would you really want to? Honestly, what if I told you that it was possible for you to release the unwanted mental and emotional attachments from the past? That you could detach to observe the past rather than feeling like you are still living in it. This is what is required for you to let go of the past, to be able to affectionately look back on it from a higher perspective and see your lessons and opportunities for growth. It also allows you to be fully present—in the present. Otherwise you will keep yourself locked into the past and subsequently holding onto your own suffering. You don't need to carry any pain from the past any longer. Of course healing takes time as you go through the process of "peeling away the layers" as they surface.

It's time to let the past go. In doing so, it may be necessary for you to "do some work" on forgiveness, compassion, and ultimately love—of yourself and others who've been in your life or crossed your path. This may also require you to release suppressed emotions such as hate, worry, grief or sadness. Or, perhaps those of fear, anxiety, anger, and resentment (these make up some of the layers!). This may be painful at first, but once you have truly healed, the internal peace that results sets you free. How you know you have healed is when you are able to remember situations or events, without the emotional attachment. Such healing work is best done with the assistance of a qualified counsellor, healer or psychologist.

Now I wish to cover the *future*!

This is an area that I get excited about, as today's thoughts, words, and actions pave the pathway for tomorrow's experiences... Ultimately whilst remaining present, we can co-create the lives of our dreams, with the Universe. Some call this manifestation!

Have you ever met someone who gets everything he or she's ever wished for? Chances are they've dreamed about living that life. Some people are able to "see" their future and even feel and know that it will transpire exactly as they imagine. Yes, your imagination is where manifestation begins.

Until I was diagnosed with bipolar, I didn't realise it was actually possible to live in the future—after all, our body is always in the present. However, as with living in the past, it *is* possible to live in the future, as you perceive it to be, once again in your mind. In early 2014, I was soon to be this successful author, on a world speaking circuit in my mind, but in reality I was an unknown writer who'd had a few speaking engagements, locally. Trust me, living in the future seriously messes with your head, creating not only possible mental disorders, but complete disharmony within yourself and your life.

If we have let go of our past, yet not reached our future, then it comes back to the *present* moment—the only time there truly is!

If we are *aware* when our minds race into the past or future, we can stop and ensure we come back to the present. This will in turn ease any anxiety symptoms (including fast heartbeat, sweating, racing thoughts, chest pressure, shortness of breath, inability to be still, and disturbed sleep). It also gives our adrenals a rest, bringing calmness and clarity of mind. It is in effect a form of meditation. So regardless of where you've been or where you're going, I invite you to be present in this *now* moment...

In this space, you will have reflected somewhat and become more aware of who you are and what you'd like. Also, what you need to let go of, change, and bring more of into your life. With that in mind, once you choose to be present and take action, you are well on your way and ready to take the next steps towards balance. So, if you choose to be that happy, healthy, joyful, confident, balanced, and loving soul with an optimistic attitude in life... it's time to look more closely at your aspects of mind, body, heart, and spirit individually, to prepare you in making some welcomed positive changes.

For personal balance;

- *Get to know yourself intimately.*

- *Be and express your true self.*

- *The answers lie within.*

- *You create the life you choose to live.*

- *Live in the present moment.*

CHAPTER 2

MIND

This chapter refers to the *mind* and is not to be confused with the brain—that forms part of the body's central nervous system. The brain is a vital physical organ and is the centre responsible for registering sensations, processing information and operating the functioning aspects of the human body.

MIND—Conscious and Subconscious
↓
Beliefs—Self-limiting and Self-supporting
↓
Thoughts (and Emotions)
↓
Words and Actions
↓
Personal Energy

Our mind communicates to us through our thoughts. Our thoughts stem from our beliefs—that stem from our (conscious and subconscious) mind. The thoughts we have often determine the words we use, and our words make up part of our individual expression (attitude) and personal energy. In order to express our higher and true selves, we are to choose our conscious thoughts and words wisely!

Begin to be aware and take note of the thoughts you have, the words and phrases you use regularly, and what you are expressing through them. There may be some expressions you like and others you don't, and they all have their own energy that goes with them. You may think and say things just because that's what others around you say. However, you are completely in charge of your thoughts and subsequent words, and only you have the power to change them. Change your thoughts, change your life... this is "the power of the mind"!

Through awareness we begin by catching any negative thoughts one by one. When you do, congratulate yourself for doing so and reframe (change) them into positive, uplifting ones that reflect the true you.

So what happens when we become consciously aware of our thoughts (and emotions)? We affirm what we believe, but something just doesn't seem right. Our thoughts don't seem to reflect that belief, or our emotions are intense or our body is responding otherwise. That's when it's time to go deeper—into our true beliefs, often hidden in the subconscious mind.

Conscious and Subconscious

Research tells us our subconscious mind is generally energetically self-programmed (like a computer) in early childhood. However, throughout life various traumatic events and certain life experiences may also cause us to lodge firm (often self-limiting) beliefs in our subconscious. Some may refer to the subconscious mind as the ego or false self.

Once we learn some things and they are programmed into our subconscious, we rarely have to think about them, it simply becomes automatic. Just think about it, you learnt to talk. Do you then need to think about talking? No. You just do it. When you first learnt to drive a car, you repeated until it became subconsciously programmed and habitual. Now you get in and drive, without so much as a thought about the process. Heck, you may even drive a couple of kilometres, totally somewhere else in your (conscious) mind, yet you were still driving and are somehow still on the road! (you were driving subconsciously, of course).

As I mentioned in the previous chapter, according to the work of Dr. Lipton, most humans operate mostly from the subconscious. Further, he states approximately 70% of the subconscious is self-limiting. However, as we become more conscious and connected to our true, higher selves, we are able to access the subconscious to reveal and heal what is holding us back.

The conscious mind is creative, intuitive, and present. Some refer to the conscious as the spiritual, soul or higher self. Unfortunately, most people are in a conscious mindset less than about five percent of the time! Meditation (and hypnosis) are valuable tools for accessing the conscious mind.

CLARE EVANS

Conscious Awareness Activity

> Can you think of a situation that has come up through your self-reflection—something you thought was a strength of conscious willpower, but you consider there could be an underlying self-limiting belief? That is a self-limiting belief that stems from your subconscious programming, and is actually holding you back?

Beliefs

We may consciously choose to believe something. However, what we are likely to be unaware of is that we may have previously subconsciously programmed ourselves to believe otherwise. For example, as an adult you may consciously think that it's fine to spend time by yourself, you are safe, and that it would be silly to think any differently. However, you may feel a little uneasy and deep down unbeknown to you, due to subconscious programming and patterning, you do not actually believe it. Due to a previous traumatic experience, you subconsciously believe that if you are left on your own, people will take advantage of you. You may also feel a little uneasy or nervous.

When this occurs what results are conflicting beliefs—that could lead to mental disorders. Dr. Lipton put it into context when he wrote, *"Tensions between conscious willpower and subconscious programs can result in serious neurological disorders"*.

Therefore, we need to become aware of our self-limiting beliefs and test our subconscious. This way we discover if there is an evident conflict between the conscious and subconscious. Then we must re-program the subconscious, to align with our conscious mind.

Great, how do we do that, I hear you say? Well, there are various ways documented that generally involve working quite intensely with a practitioner or therapist—who may be able to assist you from a detached compassionate perspective. Depending on the practitioner and method, it may take a little time to reveal some of your core self-limiting beliefs, and their subsequent release. Of course, the more open and receptive you are to healing, the more profound the results.

There are various methods of testing your energy field, including quartz pendulum (a light, even weighted crystal that suspends from a short chain) testing and muscle testing. What I discovered through my work as a holistic healer, is that your personal energy doesn't lie. It is the truth-teller of your being and why I love working with it so much! For an example, you may think and consciously believe that ice-cream is a food that is fine for you to consume. Yet, when your energy is tested for ice-cream through the various methods, it may reveal a "no" reading, an imbalance. That is basically an energetic subconscious rejection to it. Therefore, the subconscious *truths* of the mind can be revealed, when testing on an energetic level.

Energy testing is best done with a practitioner or partner, someone who is detached. This is unless you are able to access a state of (pure) consciousness. Remember that most people are in a conscious mindset less than about five percent of the time. You must also be willing to let go and surrender completely, to be a clear channel for truth. Your energy testing partner will need to ensure he or she holds the intention of being a clear channel for the truth too, in order to provide an accurate reading.

Below is a process I developed for transforming subconscious self-limiting beliefs. It can be done on your own, with a partner or with the assistance of a practitioner. This process requires you, as the person being tested, to surrender completely, become a clear channel of truth, and also be open and receptive to healing. It is best carried out in an undisturbed, quiet, and calm environment where you'll be able to retain focus and clarity.

In order to complete the process, you will need to be aware of the self-limiting belief you wish to heal. You are also required to identify the contrary self-supporting belief, one you choose to believe for a more present, balanced life.

(SELF-LIMITING) BELIEF TRANSFORMATION PROCESS

© Clare Evans 2014

1) Conscious **AWARENESS**—of possible self-limiting belief.

   (eg, I am unconfident)
   Write down the associated self-*supporting* belief (what you choose to believe):
   (eg, I am confident)

   _____

2) Determine a clear "yes" and "no" response with a pendulum (or muscle testing).
   The pendulum will swing or circle a certain way to indicate "yes", and a different way to indicate "no".
   Muscle testing will hold strong to indicate "yes", and be weak to indicate "no".

a) Name *(state, "my name is X")* (determines "Yes" response)   Y/N

b) False name *(state, "my name is Y")*(determines "No" response)   Y/N

3) **Energy TEST the subconscious level of the self-supporting belief (that you are choosing to believe consciously), with a pendulum (or muscle testing).**

a) Self-supporting belief *(state eg, "I am confident")*   Y/N

If "Yes", this indicates an alignment—your subconscious supports your conscious belief! If "No", continue to step 4.

4) **Heal and RELEASE the subconscious belief.** (This step can be completed with the assistance of a partner, therapist or counsellor, or pre-recorded on audio, so you can allow the focus to be on the healing).

a) Relax into a meditative "no-mind" space.

b) *State,* ***"I now choose and trust, the complete release, of all associated self-limiting beliefs, to occur on all levels of my being, and in all directions of time and space."***

c) Take a deep breath, relax and be willing to let go and surrender completely.

d) Energy shift occurs (usually over 2-5 minutes), to clear the self-limiting belief. The pendulum will change from "No" to "Yes", once the shift has occurred.

(Optional) record any responses of mind, body, heart or spirit: _____

_____

e) **If muscle testing**, after 2 - 5 minutes, **RE-TEST.**   Y/N

If "Yes", this indicates an alignment—your subconscious supports your conscious belief! Continue to step 5. If "No", repeat the process at another time.

5) **RE-AFFIRM** (self-supporting) belief:
   State, "I am now free, and choose to truly believe (belief)

_____

* * * * * * * * *

Yes, it can be that simple! However, the key is conscious awareness, as well as being completely open and receptive to the deep mind healing. Once you begin to clear out the old, perhaps cluttered self-limiting beliefs of the subconscious mind, you become free to be who you truly are!

A "no" answer at the conclusion of step 4, simply indicates blocked energy from a firmly held subconscious belief. If this occurs, don't be hard on yourself, and give yourself some time before repeating the process again. Everything happens as it's meant to, and it appears that now is not be the best time for the shift. Self-reflection on the belief itself, as well as the possible fear surrounding the release, may reveal more awareness and information to you. Alternatively, working with a therapist may assist you to a space that you feel safe to let go and ultimately heal the belief. The good news is that this self-limiting belief has now come into your conscious awareness—that is the first step to healing.

So now you have identified where your thoughts and words come from and how it came to be. You can begin to see how your thoughts and emotions, and subsequent attitudes and behaviour (or personal energy) are likely to be a reflection of those who were around you during your most influential and informative years.

No matter what your early journey history has been, you are in complete control of your own life. In each moment (the *now*), you are free to choose if you wish to retain those beliefs, or if you wish to transform them into fresh new self-supporting ones!

Beliefs Activity

> Spend a little reflective time to yourself now, and in your journal write down some of the self-limiting beliefs you are consciously aware of. Perhaps also include some that you may like to test your subconscious mind for, to find out if you truly believe them or not.
>
> You may also wish to focus upon what you do choose to believe, and test those beliefs too. This will enable you to ascertain if there are any "blockages" from the subconscious that may hinder your progress.
>
> Then consider clearing out what does not serve your highest good, through the *(Self-Limiting) Belief Transformation Process* for Absolute Personal Transformation.

> **Beliefs**—Self-limiting (and self-supporting), stemming from my subconscious and conscious mind:
>
> → influence my **thoughts (and emotions)**:
>
> → influence my **words and actions**, expressing my personal energy:

Can you see more clearly how your beliefs, as well as your thoughts and emotions directly influence your words and actions? More importantly, if you were to look at this concept from the perspective of words and actions, you may be able to determine some deep self-limiting beliefs. You may even be able to identify specific events or situations where a particular belief originated, and you have then programmed into your subconscious.

Beliefs Activity II

Once again, take some time for self-reflection.

Focus first on some of the *words* you use regularly. In your journal, write down three. Notice if they are positive, or perhaps harsh.

Now turning your attention to some of the *actions* you perform regularly, write down three. Again notice, are they fast and irregular, or more slow and specific?

Go deeper into the associated *thoughts* to those words and actions. Write them down.

Go deeper into the associated *emotions* to those words and actions, and write them down too.

Look closely for the *key descriptive opinions and feelings* that precede the words you use, and the actions you take.

Now focussing briefly on those "keys", and with your eyes closed, take yourself into a calm, centred space. Then ask yourself to present to you consciously, an associated self-limiting belief. Take your time and simply allow the answer to come forth.

This activity enables the possibility for you to bring to light subconscious self-limiting beliefs that you have not previously been consciously aware of. If you identify any "blockages" from the subconscious that may be hindering your progress, you can consider taking yourself (or with the assistance of someone else), through the *(Self-Limiting) Belief Transformation Process* outlined above, to clear them out.

You then regain your freedom to consciously choose to believe, think, feel, speak, and act differently—in a way that is self-supporting.

My personal energy, expressed through my **words and actions:**

↓ deeper to my **thoughts (and emotions):**

↓ deeper to significant **events or situations:**

↓ deeper to my (self-limiting) **beliefs**, stemming from my subconscious mind:

Awareness, awareness, awareness! That is key. Train yourself to "catch" yourself when you think, feel, do or state something negative.

Then re-frame (affirm) it into being a positive, optimistic, and self-supporting thought, emotion or statement. This is another way to re-program the subconscious, though it may take a little longer, especially if your subconscious believes that "practice makes perfect".

However, you can say affirmations until the cows come home (and they can be very effective on their own), but unless you acknowledge, accept, and release the presenting words and actions, thoughts, and emotions, you are effectively putting a bandaid on your own suffering. True holistic healing is deep, and comes from healing the symptom, the ailment, and most importantly the cause!

When digging deep and healing the mind, we may re-discover some of the pain from the past. Many of us "bury" significant and traumatic "stuff" as we age, building up our congestive layers. When such pain arises, we are to breathe through it, to remain present. The body is *always* in the present moment, and deep belly breathing brings us back to presence. We must be aware of perceiving and interpreting from where we are in the now, despite the pain we may currently be experiencing. This in truth is purely a reflection of what it once was. Sometimes we dig for what needs healing, but more often than not, old stuff surfaces on its own. If we surrender and breathe into our layers, as they come to the surface, this "old stuff" may be healed and released—for good!

Through my firsthand experience, here is an example;

I was overwhelmed by the emotional intensity that I felt following my first "non-publishing" experience in 2014. I consciously believed that I was an impending, published author. The work was done, all the signs were there and it seemed a miracle that a traditional publishing house was actually going to publish my little eBook. Happy days!

However, when the deal went sour and we went our separate ways, I was left feeling deeply confused, unworthy and rejected... utterly and completely devastated! The pain was excruciating. I was desperately holding on, not wanting to accept the loss or move on. I quickly fell into a major depression. Subsequently, upon psychiatric assessment I was delivered my bipolar diagnosis.

Thereafter, upon very deep reflective healing work, I was astounded to discover that that current situation with the publishing deal was simply mirroring some extremely old, unhealed emotions, and deeper—to the associated subconscious self-limiting beliefs.

Even after thirty-five years, my subconscious mind was alerting me. Through my current thoughts and emotions, I once again felt the traumatic pain that I had experienced and carried from the time my parents separated, when I was two years old.

Through allowing myself to consciously acknowledge my thoughts and fully feel my emotions, I effectively dissolved the pain of the past. Then through further exploration, I healed my inner child's associated subconscious beliefs, transforming them into conscious, self-supporting ones.

I was then able to integrate my (inner child) subconscious mind with my (adult self) conscious mind, and soon saw that publishing situation for what it was, without the pessimistic thoughts or intense feelings of confusion, unworthiness and rejection. Plus, that obviously wasn't my time to become a published author—the Universe had other plans!

If we resist such opportunities for healing and cover them up "with a bandaid", they soon become triggered and present again at another time—for another healing opportunity. Yes, it will be a continuous cycle that repeats until it is truly healed. You may not be ready to choose to delve into healing, and that's ok. However, through choosing to do so you release yourself from what holds you down and back in life. Otherwise those layers generally get thicker and heavier over time.

Please remember that conflict between the conscious and subconscious mind can lead to serious neurological and psychological disorders. A healing alternative is through letting go of old self-limiting beliefs, and consciously choosing self-supporting beliefs. This allows us to feel healthy, light, and free, and we regain our balance.

True mind healing allows us to live more consciously, creatively, and intuitively. We begin to mentally let go of what we can't control, and focus upon what we can. Aligning a healed mind and the heart allows us to forgive others with ease for their wrong doings, keeps our hearts full of compassion and love, and our minds clear. When we live more consciously we make decisions in line with our souls, and our thoughts become one of the driving forces behind our personal passions, our work/careers, and all of our relationships. We can then embrace our true, higher selves, our infinite capacity, and can really dream big in the now. Following our intuitive guidance, those dreams become manifested into our future pathway, allowing us a life of balance and wellbeing.

After working through the activities and reflecting on the concepts we have touched on, you should be getting a sense of where mind and spirit overlap. The mind and heart emotions, stemming from the subconscious, also overlap and the spaces where this happens have a rippling effect on the physical body.

For mind balance;

- *Be positive and optimistic, yet realistic, grounded, and practical.*

- *Engage in mind stimulating activities that you like.*

- *Be aware of your thoughts.*

- *Review and re-assess your life regularly.*

- *Dream, visualise, and meditate.*

- *Connect with your inner wisdom.*

- *Work and create when inspired.*

- *Become aware of and heal self-limiting beliefs, from the subconscious.*

CHAPTER 3

BODY

The brain is a vital physical organ of your human *body*—that plays a role in development, functioning and maintenance.

Your body is your vehicle in life and who knows what's along the road ahead…Just like a motor vehicle get us "from A to B" and needs to be in good working order, so too does your body. If you neglect your "vehicle" and it's not maintained; you put in dirty fuel, don't drive it very often, and don't put any air in the tyres, it may well run for some time. Yet, eventually wear and tear occurs and then your vehicle needs a lot of work for it to get back to optimal operation. Just like a car reveals what requires attention, our bodies communicate to us through our physical sensations, commonly referred to as symptoms.

Pay attention to the physical sensations of your body. Like with the thoughts, words, and actions, you have to pay full attention to your physical body. Breathe and take note. Do you have any symptoms right now? If so, what is your body attempting to communicate to you? Ascertain the message behind the symptom, so you can begin to heal the cause.

There are a few excellent books that give an insight into what your body may be trying to tell you, and I have listed them under recommended reading in *Chapter 7—A Little More Help*. These books make an excellent and valuable reference. You'll soon find yourself paying attention, raising your level of awareness, and listening to what your body is saying. Then by combining your observations with the insights to be found in the references, you can heal so much more than just your physical body. An example is; you have a pain in your left knee. Pain can refer to guilt. Left side of the body often refers to the feminine, mother, past (if you are right handed). Knee issues can be a reflection of stubborn ego and pride, inflexibility, and refusing to give in. This type of referencing provides us with extremely valuable insights into the likely metaphysical origin (that many people aren't aware of or overlook) of our physical ailments.

Of course there are times when your body has symptoms that have occurred from the outside in, like an accident that results in a broken arm for instance. In reality there are no accidents, but "synchronicities"—everything is as it's meant to be (although unfortunate to result in such an injury for the individual!). In this example, you might look up arm, right or left side of the body, and bones, to ascertain your body's message. The actions that are a remedy for healing will emerge from your level of awareness and suggestions from experienced others. Be open and completely honest with yourself, and use your intuition to determine the underlying cause (and necessary remedy) for healing from the various suggestions read. You might or might not be surprised by what you discover and learn about yourself!

Look after your body with the care it deserves and it will assist you greatly to live a long healthy life. In order for you to have a balanced and healthy body you require clothing, shelter, food, water, sun, air, and exercise.

Eat wholesome natural foods. Drink pure clean water. Breathe fresh air into your lungs. Exercise regularly. Take some time out to rest.

Eating Wholesome Natural Foods

Reality check... *"diets" do not work!*

Let's face it, if you eat a standard Western diet, there is a fair chance you may be overweight. If you are overweight, what is required is not a typical "weight loss diet" but rather a *dietary lifestyle change*! Otherwise, once you've reached your goal weight and the diet is finished, you'll more than likely return to your old eating patterns and so too will the requirements for your big clothes! The way we eat varies at each stage of our life. Some simple guidelines are;

- · *Leave treats as treats,* (rather than everyday foods)!
- · *Eat when you are hungry* and *pay attention to your portion sizes.*
- · *Eat until you are satisfied,* (rather than full).

If you are an emotional eater, please *refrain from using food as a tool to fix or feed your emotions* (my suggestion is to read the chapters on *Mind, Heart,* and *Spirit* instead)!

Children and teenagers are growing and producing more cells in their body. Therefore, at perhaps the most significant time in their lives, it's important to ensure that they receive the quality nutrients that they require for good health. As adults however, we have completed the growth stage of our lives and most likely require less calories (unless we are athletes or highly active individuals, burning more calories than we consume). Bad eating habits and excess calorie intake can cause us to gradually gain weight as we age.

Basically, we require roughly the same amount of consumed calories or kilojoules as we do expended calories or kilojoules, for weight maintenance. No matter if you are super skinny, "healthy weight for height" or obese, if you consume *more* calories than you exert, you will most likely gain weight. If you consume *less* calories than you exert, you will most likely lose weight. Just because you are skinny, doesn't necessarily mean you are healthy, and the same goes for those who are slightly overweight, that doesn't necessarily mean they are unhealthy either. The point of difference for optimal health, is in the *quality* of the nutrients you consume, per calorie!

Every person's body is different and may require different levels of vitamins and minerals, as well as abstinence of specific foods (allergies and intolerances) at different times. This is why specific advice is not given here. Choose a wide variety of the foods your body needs and tolerates. *If you don't feel good after you've eaten something or you notice some symptoms, pay attention, as your body is trying to tell you something.*

Ringing a bell, awareness is once again the key, just as you have with your mind. Keeping a food diary can assist with what foods are and aren't good for you. Write down everything you eat and see how you feel afterwards. If you notice any patterns, then adjust your diet accordingly. You could always energy test your response to specific foods too. Consult a professional if required or if you wish to have a diet plan specifically for you. There are also some references listed in *Chapter 7—A Little More Help*.

Healthy eating is not rocket science... it's basics... so let's get back to basics... vitamins, minerals, protein, carbohydrates, and (good) fat. These can all be found in nature. *Choose to eat a well balanced diet of fresh natural wholesome foods (preferably organic,* as often the soil that conventional fruits and vege are grown in, contains much less nutrients). This means mostly veges and fruit, that are full of fibre. A little meat, chicken or fish if you choose, or beans are an excellent plant-based choice! Eat wholegrains and omega 3 fats (not only in oily fish, but also found in nuts and seeds).

Most of your vitamins and minerals come in the form of fruit and vegetables (so there's a reason we're told to eat at least two fruit and five vege!)

Refrain from consuming processed and refined foods with additives and preservatives wherever possible. Some additives and preservatives, including suspected carcinogens are banned in other countries, yet are still allowed in our foods!?

Our health system has become overburdened and the standard Australian diet (SAD) is starting to be questioned by many. It's time to let go of how many of us were taught to eat and the unhealthy eating habits that we may have created! Thankfully people are slowly beginning to open up to and assimilate new ways of eating. They are realising that their health and wellbeing depends on it.

It takes twenty-one days to change a habit and small changes will be the most sustainable. Awareness, small changes, and then more changes can be made. It took me four years to move from a SAD, including meat, cheese, bread, pasta, and milk, to consuming a whole food "plant-based" diet. I became aware that there is a focus on needing more "real foods"—fruits and veges, in our diets. Though what may be more important is what needs to be taken *out* of our diets. Something else to consider is that we likely consume more than enough protein, carbohydrates, and fats.

Taking vitamin and mineral supplements will never make up for an unhealthy diet. By consuming a variety of fresh, whole, unprocessed foods (and lots of them—think again fruits and vege!), our bodies get more of the necessary vitamins, minerals, fibre, and phytochemicals, that they need. Make it a priority to review your current food consumption and decipher what positive changes you choose to make, today. Being healthy is perhaps the greatest wealth—for your health, happiness, and longevity!

Following my cancer experience, I made the transition from consuming a SAD to become a *"nutritarian"* as I strived towards optimal health and wellbeing. I'm pleased to say that I am now happier and healthier for that choice! So, what does being a nutritarian actually mean, and what is the H=N/C concept that goes with that particular eating style?

The term *nutritarian*, coined by Dr Joel Fuhrman, describes a person who follows the H=N/C formula, incorporating a variety of micro-nutrient rich plant foods (that contain phytochemicals, antioxidants, and many other beneficial compounds), and they also avoid highly processed foods. A nutritarian strives for nutritional excellence through a plant-based diet. They eat high on the nutrient density line.

The nutrient density line in descending order is; dark leafy green vegetables, other green vegetables, other non-green vegetables, fruit, beans, nuts and seeds, starchy vegetables, whole grains and white potatos, fish, fat free dairy, eggs, wild meat and chicken, full fat diary, red meat, refined grain products, cheese, refined oils, refined sweets.

Therefore, a nutritarian generally consumes more greens and less of everything else. For example; a large salad every day, at least 1/2 cup of beans/legumes, at least 3 fruits, at least 1 oz (~ 28 g) of nuts and seeds, and a large serve of green vegetables to make up ~ 90% of what they consume.

Whilst this may seem daunting and even near on impossible for many, it doesn't have to be. A nutritarian diet basically means eating mostly whole plant-based foods through a variety of different fruits and vegetables. You can begin to make positive changes for your health by taking small steps—consider starting off by replacing just one daily meal with a highly nutritious one! Perhaps by making and consuming a delicious and nutritious green smoothie for breakfast, or vege-stock based vegetable soup for your winter lunches. With just a little preparation, make a big pot to last the week, with a variety of vegetables including; garlic, onion, carrot, celery, mushrooms, broccoli, pak choy, kale, capsicum, spinach, silverbeet, and parsley. Also include a little brown rice and a (drained and rinsed) tin of mixed beans. Maybe some organic rye bread on the side too. Yummo! Now that's *real* fast food!

Dr Fuhrman's H=N/C formula is a nutrient density concept, that equates to **health** = **nutrients per calorie**. It means that your health is determined by the number of nutrients you obtain, divided by the amount of calories you consume. All calories come from fat, carbohydrates, and protein. They are *macro*-nutrients (as is water). Non-caloric compounds in food are called *micro*-nutrients.

Micronutrients are comprised of vitamins, minerals, fibre, and phytochemicals, and they are essential for optimal health. Many consuming a SAD obtain an abundance of macronutrients (carbohydrates, fats, and proteins), but not nearly enough micronutrients in our diets needed for health, disease prevention and some disease reversal.

Therefore, the formula H=N/C means that for optimal health, through the foods we eat, we must obtain the maximum amount of micro-nutrients to the amount of macro-nutrients (calories). By eating this way we can prevent many diseases and even reverse some—like type 2 diabetes and cardiovascular disease!

Dark leafy greens contain the most nutrients per calorie and include; kale, spinach, collard greens, beet greens, and broccoli. On the odd occasion that I feel a dip in my immunity, I immediately reach for the greens (and I usually realise that my consumption has lessened or I may have consumed just spinach more than any other greens). It's by mixing up the greens and rotating them that we best assimilate a variety of their nutritional properties. They really are *super* greens! No wonder big animals like gorillas grow so big and strong, and it seems Popeye was right about that spinach too!

For an added immunity boost to complement your greens, consume your G-BOMBS each day, as per Dr Fuhrman's suggestion;

> **G** - Greens
> **B** - Beans
> **O** - Onions
> **M** - Mushrooms
> **B** - Berries
> **S** - Seeds

Generally the more refined a food is, the lower it's nutrient density. Whole flaxseeds are a good example as they retain the fibre, vitamins, minerals, and phytochemicals in comparison to refined flaxseed oil. So to follow the H=N/C formula, you'd choose whole flaxseeds over flaxseed oil, and grind them down as you need them. (The same goes for coconuts and coconut oil.)

Some consuming a SAD eat mostly calories from refined and processed foods—that contain little micro-nutrients. Their H=N/C result would be far less than would a nutritarians, and subsequently they'd experience poorer health. So what are phytochemicals?

Phytochemicals are health promoting compounds (chemicals/ nutrients) found in plants and are sometimes called phyto-nutrients. They are important for good health as they reduce the risk of developing certain diseases. For example, consuming phytochemicals found in garlic and tomatos may reduce the risk of developing cancer, and grapes contain phytochemicals that may reduce the risk of heart disease.

Diseases like obesity, heart disease, diabetes, and cancer have become endemic and place an unnecessary strain on health care systems. When I had my own cancer experience seven years ago, I honestly thought my diet was pretty good and it was. I now know however, it was still too heavy in fats, carbs, and proteins. The past is the past and fortunately I am better informed about nutrition now, (that I'm now choosing to pass onto you!), including that phytochemicals potentially **prevent cancer** by;

- detoxifying and deactivating cancer causing agents and blocking the process to DNA damage.
- fuelling cellular repair of DNA damage.
- stopping the duplication of cells with DNA damage.
- protecting DNA from further damage.
- stopping the spread of cancerous cells.

For further information and how these scientific conclusions have been reached, please refer to the research work of Dr Fuhrman, as listed under the references section at the back of this book.

Some examples of foods that are high in phytochemicals include;

- Cruciferous vegetables (contain "phytos" called glucosinolates and isothiocyanates)—best cut, crushed, and chewed well, for maximum benefit. Eg; broccoli, cabbage, brussel sprouts, kale, and watercress.

- Legumes (contain phytos called isoflavones and phytosterols). Eg; beans, peas, lentils, and soybeans.

- Carotenoids (contain phytos lutein, zeaxanthin, and lycopene). Eg; red, orange, and yellow coloured fruits and vegetables. Eg; carrot, capsicum, tomato, and dark leafy greens (chlorophyll then gives them the green colour and they have the highest nutrient content, per calorie of all foods—so I suggest you eat and enjoy lots and lots of them!).

- Flavonoids Eg; berries, tea, and citrus fruits.

So basically, food really is thy medicine! By eating a large quantity and *variety* of fruits and veges every day, you get more of the much needed vitamins, minerals, fibre *and* phytochemicals (that can't be replicated in supplement form to the extent of whole plant-foods!) that *your* body needs for optimal health! To ensure you consume an abundance of leafy greens in your diet, aim to eat a large mixed leaf green salad everyday, and make it the main dish, rather than on the side. Also, a great way to start the day is with my personal favourite, a "green smoothie"!

Please ensure that as you increase the "good" fats to your diet, (rather than *adding* to any saturated fat you may already consume) it actually *replaces* the "bad" saturated fat (eg, replace butter with fresh avocado). Otherwise you may consume too many calories... and we all know what that means if it's not burnt off!

* *Tip—when mixing avocado with salad, absorption and bioavailability of the raw veges is increased! Not only will it add vitamins, nutrients, and phytochemicals, but absorb more cancer-fighting nutrients from the salad. Avocado is also a source of betasterol—that lowers cholesterol.*

Dr Fuhrman's book *Eat to Live* (ETL) changed my life for the better! Not so much was it about rapid weight loss for me when I first read it six years ago, but more a desire for improved health on a vegan-style diet. I recommended this book to my clients and here, to you too. No more starving yourself through dieting, this is about providing your body with the *nutrition* it needs— through real whole foods. By following Dr Fuhrman's guidelines and striving towards optimal health, weight loss merely becomes a welcomed side effect!

I'd like to share with you a summary of Dr Fuhrman's guidelines for the six week, rapid weight loss plan that can be found in *Eat to Live*;

> **Unlimited**—eat as much as you want!
> All raw vegetables (aim for at least 500g daily).
> Cooked green and non-green nutrient rich vegetables. (nutrient rich veges incl; eggplant, mushroom, red capsicum, onion, tomato, carrot, and cauliflower) (aim for at least 500g daily).

Beans, legumes, bean sprouts, and tofu (aim for at least 1 cup daily). *This is your meat replacement!*
Fresh fruits (at least 4 daily).

Limited
Cooked starchy vege and wholegrains (incl. squash, corn, potato, rice, sweet potato, bread, and cereal) (No more than 1 serve or 1 cup daily).
Raw nuts and seeds (no more than 30g daily).
Avocado (no more than 60g daily).
Dried fruit (max 2 tbsp daily).
Ground flaxseeds (max 1 tbsp daily).
Tip—add to your green smoothies!

Off-limits—sorry, but you'll be thankful later!
Processed foods
Dairy
Animal products
Between meal snacks
Fruit juices
Oils
Tip—that's where soups are ideal—no need to add oil!

Please be aware that if you choose to follow Dr Fuhrman's plan, you may experience detoxification symptoms as your body begins cellular repair and rids itself of excess weight, toxins, and wastes. Headaches and fatigue are likely—especially in the first few days, but will generally pass after a few weeks. Listen to your body—rest as much as possible when tired and remember that "this too shall pass". Please be very kind to yourself, especially during the first few days.

Of course there is a lot more wonderful scientific based nutritional information in *Eat to Live*, as well as all of Dr Fuhrman's other books, that you'll find on his website and blog. I hope you choose to become even more informed, to start healing your body and improving your health, beginning today!

The first step is to *get rid of any food addictions* and begin to eat a plant-based diet high in micro-nutrients, perferably organic. Take some time to prepare a specific menu and shopping plan. Ideally you'd shop twice per week for fresh produce. Cook a large pot of *(veges with beans, legumes or wholegrains in low-salt vege stock)* soup each week and prepare and cook vegetables a couple of times per week in winter. Store your soup in sealed glass containers in the refrigerator to retain the nutrients, and gently reheat to below boiling as required. Pre-packing food for school and work will ensure you have time to do approximately four hours of exercise per week too.

Simply adding fruits and vege to our diets is not enough and may lead to consuming too many calories—and weight gain. We need to *replace* dense calorie foods with nutritious ones that include vitamins, nutrients, and phytochemicals.

What's required is a *conscious choice*, to cut some of the damaging foods from our diets! Therefore, rather than looking at what you could be eating more of, first we must look at what to replace.

If you think about recommendations for pregnant women—it's not ok for them to eat certain things to ensure the health of them and their unborn child, so what makes us think it's ok for the rest of us to consume those foods reguarly?

Would you like to introduce yourself to a nutritarian diet lifestyle?

Here are some tips to get you started;

1. If you haven't done so already—*consider eliminating or dramatically reducing the following*;

    Butter, cheese (yes, cheese!), potato chips, doughnuts, salt, sausages, and bbq meat—too much saturated fat and little nutrition.

2. Consider also *reducing* the following;

    Refined white flour products, including white bread, pasta, and sweets—choose whole grains instead.

    Animal products, including meats and milk—choose beans as a plant-based protein.

    Full fat dairy—perhaps consider choosing low-fat varieties, but beware of added sugar in low-fat yoghurts.

    Refined sweets—chocolate is not a health food—however, it is one of those special treats and I'm definitely not suggesting you never have it again, just choose quality over quantity *and* reduce the quantity!

    Refined oils—contain little nutrients and is basically 100% fat.

    Alcohol—I understand this is a big ask, especially in our Western culture, but it's just empty calories and full of toxins.

Coffee—many people seem to have a love affair with coffee these days and it seems to have become so socially acceptable, despite being full of caffeine.

Cigarettes and social drugs—although not a food as such, these toxins are best not put into our bodies!

* * * * * * * *

Aim to make the salad the main dish and if you just *love* your cheese, as many do, perhaps consider switching to a low fat variety before you make the big decision to cut it out entirely. Also, you may want to re-think temptations like ham and cheese croissants, cakes or other low nutrient dense foods, and eat mindfully—ask yourself, "Is what I'm choosing to eat *harmful* or *healing*?"

You may choose to cut or reduce only one element of your diet, and even that one small change is such a fantastic, positive step! Congratulations, you are choosing to make a wise decision to improve your health and your life. If you take two steps forward and one step back, let it go and be kind to yourself by shifting your focus back to respecting and nurturing your body, through nutrition. Elicit the support of family and friends, and enjoy getting healthy and creative in the kitchen!

Once your changes have been maintained for a while, you may then like to remove something else and continue on a journey of self-healing and repair for your vehicle in life—your precious body!

There is so much information out there—especially on the internet! A lot claim to be researched or evidential, but against what? Just because a food is more beneficial than others, doesn't necessarily mean it's healthful. There are so many variables and no two people are the same. What is important is to seek what resonates with you, and being aware of how you feel when you read something or when you make specific dietary changes. Your health is in your hands and you are the only one who controls what goes into your mouth.

We are wise to utilise a combination of traditional medicine and natural healthcare. Doctors well understand the body, disease, and medicinal drugs that treat the symptoms of disease. However, these drugs may only provide a bandaid approach and very well not be treating the underlying cause. May I suggest that if your medical doctor is not supportive of the intuitive direction you wish to take with regards to your diet and health, seek a health professional who will be happy to assist? There are many out there!

The choice is yours on who you will allow to provide assistance with your health and wellbeing. Remember that by listening to your body you will know yourself better than anyone else. Also, not everything you see, read or hear about diet and nutrition is necessarily the truth.

Typical withdrawal symptoms generally are the short term result of purifying your diet. Therefore, if you have been inspired to clean up your diet recently (a positive dietary change!) chances are you've experienced some of the following withdrawal symptoms too;

- lethargy—low energy.
- headache.
- brain-fogginess—inability to think clearly.
- feeling nauseous.
- moodiness.

The good news is that your body had the chance to heal by releasing stored toxins and repairing its cells.

Some helpful tips to get through the first few days of detoxing are;

- let your family, friends and colleagues know you will be detoxing and elicit their support.
- keep exercise gentle, like walking.
- rest when you can—particularly if tired.
- drink pure water.
- resist the temptation of taking pain medications.
- keep going—know that it won't last and you are doing your body, mind, heart, and spirit the world of good!

If you experience any of the above mentioned detoxification symptoms longer than a couple of days please consult your medical practitioner, as soon as possible. Generally after a few days you will be feeling better than before you made the changes. More importantly you are making a positive step (provided you do not return to old habits!) towards optimal health and disease *prevention!* Soon you will have more energy, be clearer of mind, and be more productive. Your digestion will improve, you'll feel happier, skin and eyes will be clearer, and your intuition will be too. Well done!

If you feel intuitively guided to consume less meat, I ask you to trust your own inner wisdom. My family and I slowly made the transition and feel so much healthier for it. Now we consume less animal products overall. Bean dishes make an excellent replacement for meat ones! Our personal favourite is chilli con carne (without chilli perhaps, for kids) with red kidney beans and lentils (in place of mince). You can often use lentils in place of mince in recipes—enjoy getting a bit creative in the kitchen. Vege and bean soups are great in winter too. By eating this way, you'll be on your way to a plant-based diet and all the benefits that brings.

The biggest suggestion I can make is that you take one step at a time and make gradual changes! By resisting the temptation to switching every meat meal to vege based and instead changing little by little, those changes will likely have your family being more receptive. Therefore, they will be longer lasting changes, and perhaps even permanent!

The next biggest suggestion is to gain some support—swap recipes with friends and each week you each find a new one to try and then share with others. Dietary changes can be a challenge, but worth it for the health and happiness of you, your family, and the entire population of the world.

Please, please, please; consult your medical physician *prior* to undertaking any major diet or lifestyle changes—especially if you are on medication, are pregnant or have a pre-existing medical condition! Also consult your medical physician should you experience the above mentioned detoxification symptoms longer than the expected time or any other concerning symptoms, at anytime.

Pure Clean Water

Most of us are aware that the average human adult body is 50 - 70% water. This varies for males and females and is also dependent on weight. Water is an essential nutrient and efficient hydration ensures we have the ability of mental clarity, fine motor control, increased attention, regular body temperature, and energy. However, did you know that the amount of water we require for adequate hydration and body functioning and repairing varies greatly between individuals, their diet, and lifestyle?

After I'd transitioned from a SAD to a plant-based diet, I found I wasn't anywhere near as thirsty as I used to be. On the odd occasion that I'd have a SAD meal that was high in refined carbohydrates, fats, and proteins (ie, spaghetti bolognese or pizza) and almost void of fruits and vegetables, I would get extremely thirsty afterwards. I required a lot more water afterwards, to make up for the lack of it in my meal. The higher the water content of your food, naturally the less thirsty you'll be. Although it is still essential that we continue to drink water, on a plant-based diet, you simply won't require as much of it (on its own). This is because you will be obtaining much of it from your higher water content foods, particularly fruits and vegetables.

Coffee and tea contain some beneficial antioxidant compounds. However, unless decaffeinated (water filtered), they also contain caffeine, a toxin, that when consumed in large doses can begin to effect your adrenals and nervous system—not ideal for those of us already experiencing anxiety symptoms. Only pure herbal and rooibus teas are naturally caffeine free. People may think that it is caffeine free, however, green tea does indeed contain caffeine (unless specifically decaffeinated). All teas contribute to water consumption.

Did you know that caffeine and animal protein are two of the dietary factors that can contribute to increased calcium loss through the urine?! Fruits and vege however, help strengthen bones! Hmm... coffee, anyone? Think about this... how do cows become such large animals and get so much calcium in their milk? They eat green grass. Yes, we are back to greens!

Leafy green veges are high in calcium as well as other vitamins, minerals, fibre, and phytochemicals. Excellent examples are kale, bok choy, broccoli, and spinach. Cos or romaine lettuce is a good lettuce choice. It's in the bitterness that we get the goodness! With time you'll learn to love greens, if you don't already, and spinach is the mildest flavour to begin with.

When it comes to tap water, it often contains alum, chlorine, and fluoride. I suggest you purchase either an under sink or a counter top filter, to remove a large portion of the chemicals and purify your drinking water.

Alcohol contains very little nutrients and "a whole lotta calories" (often referred to as empty calories). As with any other personal choices, deciding on whether or not to drink alcohol is your decision, and yours alone. Not drinking when most others are can feel very alienating, especially if you've grown up around or are accustomed to social drinking. The learnt habit can be challenging to break. I transitioned away from drinking over time, much as my diet changed as well and it was very helpful to elicit the loving support of some non-drinking friends! My drink of preference mostly goes back to pure clean water—yet in a social setting it's nice to enjoy it with a wedge of lemon!

Time in Nature—Sunshine and Fresh Air

When we spend time outdoors we obtain valuable vitamin D from the sun as well as oxygen rich air, both essential for health.

Due to so much time spent indoors many are vitamin D deficient. If your health needs some fine tuning, it would pay to have your vitamin D levels checked at the next visit to your doctor and supplement if necessary.

Clean, oxygenated air is the purest in nature, as plants (absorb our carbon dioxide and) release oxygen. Places like the country, beaches, forests, and nature reserves are ideal sources of oxygen dense air. A few deep breaths whilst spending time there regularly is extremely beneficial for your health and wellbeing. Deep breathing oxygenates the blood and moves the lymph around your body. It also increase your chi (also called prana or life force) energy!

Stuck in the City? Indoor plants like spathiphyllum (peace lily) will also oxygenate the air inside your home. When the weather permits, open up the windows and doors to circulate the air. Also, exercise outdoors in nature when possible. Most cities have nature reserves and parks dotted throughout, so get back to nature by locating your nearest favourite and visit there often.

Regular Exercise

Again, you are an individual. For some exercise comes naturally, for others it feels like a chore. Choose exercise specifically suited to you!

I firmly believe that exercise is not negotiable, particularly if you work an inactive job and/or lead a sedentary lifestyle. Exercise alleviates depression and anxiety, releases endorphins (feel good hormones), and stimulates the heart to circulate blood around your body—delivering oxygen and nutrients (from the healthy diet you are eating!). Exercise also stimulates the lymph to remove wastes and toxins, tones muscles, and strengthens bones. Also, it boosts serotonin in your brain, boosts immunity, improves sleep, helps prevent disease, and helps maintain weight. Gee, the benefits really are plentiful!

Perhaps you could also consider treating yourself each month to a therapeutic hands-on body treatment, like massage that holds benefits similar to gentle exercise.

Even if it's wet and a little windy and cold outside, does that stop you from exercising? Heck, *no*! Not if you choose to commit to self, a daily exercise regime and find the joy in taking even just a brisk half hour walk, during winter. Just remember to take an umbrella with you!

Perhaps you are still lacking a little *motivation for winter exercise*? Here are some tips that may assist you;

- *Music*—I've never met anyone who doesn't like music in one form or another. Get the latest tunes or your old favourites on your iPod/Phone or electronic device and get moving! Shuffle will keep it interesting as will changing your playlists regularly.

- Choose the *time of day that best suits you*. For some it will be dark when they leave for work and dark when they get home, but the low light can be an excuse. If necessary do indoor activities and do bulk of your exercise on the weekend. For others, we are able to utilise the mid-day to afternoon maximum temperatures. That will make outdoor activities more comfortable and enjoyable.

- Exercise *with someone else*—committing to exercise with another person will likely keep *you* committed, as does a gym membership. If you don't want company or to talk to anyone, perhaps you, a neighbour or a friend has a dog?! I know he or she'll love a good work out with you!

- *Indoors*—there are heaps of ways to exercise indoors like;

  Swimming, dance, work out DVD, yoga, skipping, pilates, qi gong, gym, squats or weights. Open up a window and let in some fresh air, and work a little harder to ensure you keep warm. Get a little creative and remember unless you have no sensation or movement in both your upper and lower body, you can always do some form of exercise activity!

- *Change it up*—rotate your activities to keep it interesting! Try an exercise you've never done before, or haven't done since childhood.

- *Make the commitment*—write it down, sign it and place it where you can see it each day.

- *Reward yourself* for your committed efforts if you've reached your exercise goals—perhaps in the form of an outing with a friend, new music or new clothes.

- *Visualisation*—imagine how you'll look and feel after your exercise today, next week, next month...

To make the most of your exercise ensure you incorporate each major area; cardiovascular or interval, strength or muscle building, flexibility, and balance. Perhaps more importantly; warm up, work within your own limitations, and remember to have fun. You could try a combination of walking, jogging, sprints, weights, resistance training, yoga, pilates, qi gong, individual sports or team sports. You'll look forward to your daily exercise and it'll be more sustainable if you enjoy it!

Exercise Commitment

In your journal, write down all the physical activities that you enjoy. Decide on a regular routine and write it down as your way of committing to it. Be specific. What, where, when, how, and why! Then choose to take specific *action*.

Time Out to Rest—Relaxation and Meditation

We frequently lead such busy lifestyles and that often means that our minds are busy too. Life can be go-go-go, yet it's imperative for our health and wellbeing that we make time for relaxation. We aren't designed to go non-stop, all day. Let's take a look again at nature, this time cats and dogs... now they certainly know how to enjoy a good nap, don't they? We would benefit greatly from following their lead and enjoying regular breaks throughout our day too.

Some physical activities like qi gong and yoga include relaxation and meditation towards the end of the session. This is why I personally *love* them. The gentle combination of mind, body, heart, and spirit into the stretching exercises will leave you feeling completely refreshed and rebalanced. If you haven't experienced yoga already, do yourself a favour and get along to a class that's suitable for you, there are many styles available, and try it for yourself.

Here's my favourite qi gong sequence, *The Eight Treasures*. You may like to try it (or again find a class to attend and you'll likely meet some new friends as an added bonus). It is simple, connective, and highly beneficial to your being.

Qi Gong – The Eight Treasures

Designed to allow energy (or qi—pronounced "chee"), to move freely through the body, Qi Gong strengthens and maintains the immune system, prevents disease and heals the body. It improves posture and encourages alignment of the spine. Stretches combined with deep diaphragm breathing allows maximum oxygen to reach the vital organs—ultimately allowing your entire being to be relaxed and balanced—of mind, body, heart and spirit.

The eight treasures is done by repeating each of the 8 sequences, 8 times each—therefore with the various stretches, you actually take 64 deep breaths! This makes for very gentle, yet effective exercise—particularly if done outdoors and in nature! Please allow approximately 30 minutes (longer for extended meditation at the end) and remember that my version may vary slightly, from other traditional Qi Gong sequences.

1. **Holding the sky with both hands** (reaching for the Universe/Divine/Heaven/God) **x 8**

   Stretches body, expands lungs, increases oxygen intake and energy.

   With fingers intertwined in front of you, at your hips, BREATHE IN and in a smooth movement, follow your hands with your eyes as you pull your hands up to your waist, and then turn them outwards and push up to reach for the sky. Reverse the movement as you BREATHE OUT, to return to your original position. Repeat eight times.

2. **Reach the hands to the feet** (reaching for the Earth/Gaia) **x 8**

   Stretches lower abdominal and back muscles, strengthens kidneys, adrenal glands, ureters, abdominal aorta, inferior vena cava and lumbar vertebrae.

   With fingers intertwined in front of you, at your hips, BREATHE IN and in a smooth movement, follow your hands with your eyes as you turn your hands over and push down (bending over as comfortably as you can go) to reach for the earth. Reverse the movement as you BREATHE OUT, to return to your original position. Repeat eight times.

3. **Opposing arm stretch** (reaching for heaven and earth) **x 8**

   Assists function of spleen and digestive system, relieves tension.

With hands together at your heart centre, BREATHE IN and in a smooth movement, follow one hand with your eyes as you push it up, and the other down, simultaneously. Reverse the movement as you BREATHE OUT, to return to your original position. Alternate hands, four times each.

4. **Turning the head and looking behind with the eyes x 8**

Increases blood circulation to the head, improves brain and nervous system function, strengthens neck and eye muscles, promotes balance of all bodies, reduces blood pressure.

With feet shoulder width apart, arms by your sides, keep your head and spine straight and BREATHE IN as you turn your head to the left and allow your shoulders and hips to follow as far as you are comfortable. BREATHE OUT as you return to your original position. Alternate looking left and right, four times each.

5. **Shaking off illness** (shifting weight to toes, then heels) **x 8**

Calms emotions, increases energy, massages reflexology points in the foot, strengthens feet and legs.

With feet shoulder width apart, arms by your sides, keep your head and spine straight and BREATHE IN as you raise yourself up onto the balls of your feet. BREATHE OUT as you shift your weight to the heels of your feet. Raise onto the balls of your feet eight times.

6   **Shaking off tension** (side stretches) **x 8**

Relieves tension, anxiety and worry. Improves brain function, calms the mind, strengthens the waist and legs.

With feet a little wider than shoulder width apart, hands on your hips and looking straight ahead, BREATHE IN as you bend to one side. BREATHE OUT as you return to your original position. Alternate left and right, four times each.

7.   **Pushing out fists to gather strength x 8**

Stimulates the muscles, nervous system and circulation, increases personal power, strength and stamina.

With feet a little wider than shoulder width apart, clenched fists at your hips, turned upwards and looking straight ahead. BREATHE IN and as you BREATHE OUT, turn over and punch one fist forward and pull the other one backwards slightly. BREATHE IN as you return to your original position. Alternate left and right, four times each.

8.   **Bow and arrow** (with side lunges) **x 8**

Assists the respiratory and circulatory systems and strengthens the chest, arm and shoulder muscles.

*With feet a little wider than shoulder width apart,
make a bow and arrow with your arms (clench fist
with pointed finger and thumb of one hand, and
clench fist of the other hand), crossed at your heart
centre and looking straight ahead. BREATHE IN
as you un-cross your arms and step out and lunge
slightly in the direction of the "arrow", pulling the
bow back slightly. BREATHE OUT as you return
to your original position and swap arms (and also
bow and arrow). Alternate left and right, four
times each.*

After completing the sequence uncross arms
and cross legs. Sit in quiet meditation for 1 –
5 minutes. If desired, follow with gathering
(stretch arms up and scoop or push into your
centre—solar plexus—at the base of your
ribcage or heart area) the energy raised from
the eight treasures, three times, and then
direct it to any area requiring healing, (place
your hands on the area or intuitively direct it
to where it's required) or at your heart centre.
Again sit quietly for a minute or two, and know
that the healing will continue, once you begin
to go about your day...

Skincare

As far as skincare goes, again aim for as natural as possible. Some
say if you wouldn't eat it, don't put it on your skin. That's going
completely natural! Not that I'd eat it, but personally I like to
use a variety of brands of skincare with aromatherapy in it, like
In Essence and *World Organic*. They're reasonably priced, smell

nice, and feel lovely on your skin too. Perhaps if you go to your local health food store and try some of their testers for different products, you might find some that appeal to you. Have a look on the ingredients lists—if it's full of big long chemical words, it's likely to be full of artificial stuff! Like everyone's diets are to be specific to their requirements, I feel skincare is pretty much the same, as we are all individuals.

What's perhaps more important than what we put on our bodies, is what we put into our bodies in the way of nutrition and also lifestyle factors. I know that along with regular exercise, the more cleanly I eat, the better my skin! Beauty from the inside, out! By now you are probably seeing how some things effect everything else just within the physical, and soon you will discover how the physical as a whole affects all of our other levels of being too.

Next we move to focus upon an area of self that for me was perhaps the most significant along my healing journey. As a highly sensitive person, the heart is where I feel I made the greatest shift, and perhaps you will too.

> *For body balance;*
>
> *- Eat wholesome, natural foods.*
>
> *- Drink pure clean water.*
>
> *- Get a little sun and breathe fresh air into your lungs.*
>
> *- Exercise regularly.*
>
> *- Take some time to rest and relax.*

CHAPTER 4

HEART

Love. We can't see it, touch it, hear it, taste it or smell it. So how do we know it's real? Because we *feel* it! Ahhh... the wonderful emotional feeling of love... everyone has felt it, at some stage! Are you aware that love can be subdivided into different types?— self-love, love that we share with others through giving and receiving, and unconditional love.

Self-love and acceptance is how we feel about and care for ourselves, and the only person who can give us self-love is obviously ourselves. Unfortunately, if we don't feel it a great deal we can be depressed, withdrawn, and don't know who we really are. This eventually starts to have an impact on our other levels, including physically. Some deeply and completely love and accept ourselves—that allows us to be full of self-love. When we are full of self-love we are usually our authentic selves, confident, happy, and optimistic. We nurture ourselves on all levels of being and give ourselves what we need—creating an inner life of health, happiness, and harmony.

Love that we share with others through giving and receiving, is love exchanged—beyond ourselves. This may be experienced through physical touch, sharing, assisting, smiling, and being our true selves in the presence of others. Also, to accept others' offers of assistance, gifts, and compliments is to receive love. If, whilst in the presence of others and they are not projecting love, we sometimes withdraw, close our hearts, and not a lot of love is exchanged. However, if we open our hearts and send love, we often receive it back—as what we give out eventually returns to us. If we treat others the way we wish to be treated, we are leading by example and giving love to others far more than we may realise. We are giving love, unconditionally.

Unconditional love is without expectations. This occurs when we love and accept ourselves and all others as they are, and our hearts remain open to love—regardless of what others project at us. We easily forgive. Our hearts are strong, that supports all other aspects of self—physical, mental, and spiritual, and we do our part in living in harmony with others and the world around us.

When we are full of love it makes us want to sing, dance, and perhaps scream for joy. We may also feel other emotions like peacefulness, contentment, confidence, empowerment, joyfulness, and happiness. When we don't feel love it can make us withdraw, hide, and perhaps cry. Therefore, sometimes we are up, others down, and this is just from one emotion! We feel many emotions throughout our days. Generally we welcome the "positive" emotions, and push away the "negative" ones. Our hearts communicate to us through our emotions—that often stem from our buried subconscious beliefs.

We feel emotions, but we are not them (love is perhaps the exception here!), and they are not necessarily "good" or "bad" either, they just "are". The good labelled emotions can feel optimistic, uplifting, and expansive, where as the bad labelled emotions can feel pessimistic, deflating, and constrictive. Feeling *emotions* of the heart (eg, happiness) is different to feeling *sensations* through the physical body (eg, cold or chilly). Both emotional feelings and physical feelings are felt through *awareness*.

Emotions are generally not a part of us, unless we hold onto or suppress them. You could imagine a suppressed emotion like a rock in your back-pack, as you go on your journey. If you don't realise you have a rock you are likely to carry on for a while, but then you might carry another rock, then another. Before you know it you are weighed down and it starts to have an impact on you. What's required is to pick out each rock when you realise it's there, and throw it away—to make your load much lighter! The more you do this, the more easily you'll know when you are carrying a rock (emotion) and need to let it go. If you are a sensitive person then emotional awareness and expression is particularly paramount. By acknowledging, accepting, expressing, and releasing emotions, you are able to let them go. That allows you to travel lightly.

Acknowledging emotions takes awareness *at the time of* the emotion. It's a matter of pausing and connecting with how you feel in that moment, and if necessary asking yourself, "How do I feel?" Give the emotion a name.

Accepting your emotions is to *own* them—they are after all, yours. You could say out loud or to yourself, "I feel..." By saying it out loud, you not only say it, but you hear yourself saying it. You then own it, but not for long—if you so choose.

Expressing your emotions is when you *connect* with them. Allowing yourself to fully feel them then gives those feelings their own identity—remembering they are not you. You may choose to express your emotions internally through rocking or crying or outwardly express them; through activities like drawing, journaling or dancing.

Releasing emotions in healthy ways is when you *choose to let them go* without affecting other things or people. This allows true emotional freedom. Once you have made the decision to let go, it is time for forgiveness. Forgiveness does not mean forgetting, yet it allows you to release the grip on your negative emotions. That in turn releases you from the pain. You set yourself free.

We know we have fully released our emotions when we can reflect upon a situation, without it triggering the emotions. Past significant events in our lives are likely to be ones we always remember, yet we are no longer affected by them and we are emotionally calm. If we still feel emotional, it is likely that we have not healed these emotions and are still holding on—we continue to carry "rocks in our back-pack".

Sometimes you may not want to let go. That is effectively choosing to hold on. Letting go is a choice only you can make, at a time when you are ready. You can choose to carry the pain, or you can choose to let it go. If there are other people involved they may or may not carry (their own) pain. You may feel others are responsible, and they may be responsible for the situation. However, the only person who is responsible for *your* emotions, is *you*.

Feelings are often messengers—if you detach and observe from the higher perspective of your true self. You are then able to become aware of what your feelings are really alerting you to in the bigger picture.

Often emotions mask deeper emotions. For example, you might easily acknowledge you feel angry. If you allow yourself to feel and go a little deeper though, you might find that the anger is actually overshadowing an emotion like sadness or fear. One weekend I found myself in this exact situation. I was asking my family for their assistance and no action was being taken—they weren't listening to me and I was feeling angry! I took myself to a quiet space, sat with my eyes closed, and allowed myself to feel it. My anger intensified then soon went away. I asked myself again, "what am I feeling?" and then came the sadness. I was feeling sad, because I was speaking and speaking, yet wasn't being heard. My release came through tears—my usual form of emotional release. Then I felt calm and was able to openly and effectively communicate my feelings and needs with my family. They responded to my requests and I gained the assistance required.

Sometimes you don't know why you feel a certain way, and the feelings don't quite seem relevant to the current situation. In this instance the emotions have likely been triggered in the present, yet stem from suppressed emotions from a previous time. These emotions require a deeper exploration to expose the core beliefs for release. If you aren't able to do this on your own, you may choose to elicit the assistance of a therapist. Occasionally we don't want to go back to those feelings for fear of further hurt. Yet, it is necessary in order to acknowledge, accept, express, and release those surfacing emotions. In doing so we release a layer, or perhaps a layer within a layer!, and progress in our healing towards emotional freedom.

For emotional freedom;		
Acknowledge	-	***awareness* of it**
Accept	-	***own* it**
Express	-	***connect* with it**
Release	-	***choose to let it go***

When something occurs in our lives, we often form specific beliefs based on that event. These beliefs ultimately lead to how we behave. These behaviours are the *consequences* of our beliefs. Therefore, our emotions are likely in alignment with our thoughts, rather than the actual event. For example, a lady has just taken up painting as a hobby and has finished a piece to enter into a competition. She likes her creation and shows her work colleague, who criticises it and says it's definitely not good enough to enter (the event). The lady begins to feel doubtful and unworthy, and she thinks her work is no good (the belief/thought). Therefore, she doesn't enter the competition (the consequence), regardless of it being a magnificent piece, worthy of winning!

Begin to gain a greater awareness of how you feel, then step back from your emotions to view from a detached perspective. Examine what event triggered the emotions, and the corresponding thoughts that *you* created. Observe how it made you feel, how you reacted, and also how your body responded. Then you can begin to change your thoughts into positive ones. That will likely change the consequences into positive ones too.

A conscious decision must be made in order to shift from possible victim to take responsibility for your life. Begin to change perceptions and break the cycles—this is where we can see the combination of the mind and heart.

Self-reflection—examining the consequences of your thoughts related to specific events.

Event: _____

Emotion/Thought/Belief: _____

Consequence: _____

What about the difference between emotions and thoughts. In order to decipher the difference, ask yourself, "Do I feel it, or am I experiencing it?" For example, do I feel a bad day, or am I having a bad day? I am having a bad day—this is a thought. As is if someone asks you "How are you feeling today?" and you answer "Busy". The response to being busy may be emotions like feeling anxious or overwhelmed, however, busy is not the emotion but rather the experience. Once you begin to have awareness of the difference between emotions and thoughts, you may discover that you are thinking more than you are feeling, or feeling more than you are thinking. Sometimes emotional feelings can be confused with physical sensations too. For example you might "feel" cold as in temperature. That refers to the physical sensation. Or you might "feel" cold as in withdrawn. That refers to the emotional feeling.

Is there a more dominant part of yourself that you express— mental, emotional, physical, or perhaps an even distribution of them?

In the Western world, the focus has been predominantly on intellectual intelligence. However, emotional intelligence is equally important. It gives us life skills and enables us to make decisions with both our minds and our hearts. Being emotionally intelligent not only means to acknowledge, accept, express, and release our emotions. It also means you are aware of yours and others' emotions, efficiently communicate with others, and respond rather than react. You'll be optimistic, realistic, empathetic, and allow others to deal with their own emotions. With emotional intelligence you understand that you are the one in control of you. You are open to healing and growth, learn from your challenging emotions and experiences, and honour your own truth and integrity. You give yourself what you need, and respect yourself and all others. Ultimately you make decisions based on both your intellectual and emotional needs. Rather than allowing your emotions to manage you, you can manage your emotions.

As a reformed emotional eater, as hard and painful as it was at the time, the greatest thing I learnt through my experience with bulimia was to step away from the chocolate and connect with my emotions! Perhaps if you are someone who finds yourself in the pantry, stuffing yourself full of food—knowing full well you are *not* hungry—stop and ask yourself, "What am I feeling?" When you "emotionally eat", the imbalance is in your heart aspect of self, that then affects your physical aspect. I've never known anyone to emotionally eat or binge on something healthy, like carrots! Another example of emotional avoidance is turning to drugs, alcohol or anything else used to masks your emotions. Start to allow yourself to be aware of when this occurs.

Some of the more challenging emotions are fear, anger, loneliness, grief, and depression. These are often the emotions hidden in our "backpacks". They are often held on to and suppressed, weighing us down and limiting us from being emotionally free. If feeling yourself start to slip into challenging emotions, take positive action to release them, preventing an emotional downward spiral. If you are unable to release emotions yourself, you may wish to elicit the assistance of a therapist. You'll find a list of therapies provided in *Chapter 7—A Little More Help.*

Fear

Fear is an emotional response to a perceived or real threat. It usually is a learnt response from what we've been taught or personal negative past experiences. For example, a fear of heights may come from being pushed off the playground equipment at pre-school age. Another example is a fear of snakes; from being told as a child, "snakes are dangerous and are full of venom that can kill you!"

Fear affects our physical bodies by triggering the "fight or flight" response via a release of adrenaline. Fear is emotional, fight or flight is physical. If we are in fight or flight mode for an intense or prolonged time, it puts the body under stress. This is also true for any intense or prolonged emotions and stress management techniques are recommended for your health and wellbeing. Stress management includes deep breathing, gentle exercise, meditation, and others. Specific techniques will be discussed more in *Chapter 6—The Balance of Being.*

The other end of the spectrum to the strong emotion of fear, is strength—that comes through love, self-trust, wisdom, and courage. You can learn to overcome fears by talking with someone you trust, focusing on the present, releasing anxieties, and letting go of what's not in your control. Also visualisation techniques, examining your beliefs, taking positive action, and even exposing yourself to the fear too. Deep healing can take place when we explore deep intense emotions, such as fear. Acknowledging profoundly strong emotions and choosing to let these go, allows for a complete release. Please also remember that therapists can assist you with this—you don't have to experience these intense emotions alone.

Anger

How we express the emotion of anger is also a learnt behaviour. When we are angry, we can withdraw from others, give the silent treatment or manipulate others—this is passive anger. If we react in an out of control behaviour, hurting ourselves and others, mentally, emotionally or physically, then we are expressing aggressive anger. If through being angry you gain awareness, strength, and confidence to respond (rather than react), outwardly express your anger in healthy ways. You are then effectively managing your emotions.

Loneliness

As a social being, if your social needs are not met you may begin to feel lonely. You may also sense disconnectedness, think that you don't belong, and that you are lost and empty. Some people are happy to be alone, without loneliness. Therefore, loneliness is different to being alone. To overcome loneliness it's important to do something that you enjoy, each day. You could also make social contact with friends or family, or treat yourself in healthy ways. For example, buy yourself a nice new top, enjoy a facial or massage, or take time out to immerse yourself in nature.

Overcoming Loneliness Activity

If you do feel lonely, spend some reflective time now, exploring and writing down what you think may have contributed to your feelings of loneliness.

Follow this with recording possible ways you can work towards overcoming that loneliness.

Then choose to take specific action, to create a positive change.

Grief

Most people think of someone dying when they think of grief, yet grief is the emotional result of loss. As well as grief for the death of a loved one, grief can also be felt from losing a job, children moving away or loss of a relationship. Grief is also often accompanied with other emotions such as helplessness, sadness, and loneliness. Regardless of the loss that creates the grief, most will move through the stages of grief as described by Swiss psychiatrist Dr. Elisabeth Kubler-Ross; denial and isolation, anger and resentment, bargaining, depression, and acceptance.

For healing, each stage needs to be addressed through awareness. Denial and isolation is when people are in shock, disbelief, and coming to terms with the reality of the situation. Anger and resentment is when people blame others or the situation for their grief. Bargaining may occur when someone wishes to go back and change the situation. Depression may occur when grief is intense and/or long. Acceptance is the final stage that allows someone to begin to heal his or her grief and move on with their life.

Some will choose to grieve internally and others externally. Everyone will do so in their own way. This for many is also a time of nurturing their spiritual aspect of self and reflecting on their faith.

Depression

Feeling helpless, sad or low are normal, common feelings and they may not be accompanied by feelings of depression. The feeling of depression however, is often accompanied with those of helplessness, sadness, and unhappiness. This combination of emotions may also begin to impact on those around you as you withdraw from them and your regular lifestyle. When feeling depressed ensure you nurture yourself, ask for assistance, and give yourself what you need. That may be time to self, resting or doing a joyful activity—to regain energy, calmness of heart, and clarity of mind. If the emotions persist or intensify, please consult your medical professional.

Depressive feelings are different to clinical depression—one might feel depressed, yet aren't clinically depressed. Clinical depression is diagnosed by a professional medical practitioner and comes with symptoms of low chemicals in the brain including serotonin and dopamine. Depression may be caused by many varying factors, none that on their own are that significant, yet when combined are. It may be short lived or extend on for years and can be accompanied with negative thoughts, negative self-image, and a lack-lustre view of living. Clinical depression then often impacts on all areas of a person's life, including their work, friendships, and social circle. For those diagnosed with clinical depression, care of self is important, but additional, professionally provided tools are required.

Regardless of the cause of clinical depression, a combination of possible medical assistance and personal choices can be integrated to begin alleviating the cause, symptoms, and the ailment. Medication only plays one part, the rest is up to you through actions such as reframed thoughts, engaging in joyful activities, and making lifestyle changes. Also eating healthily and making time for regular exercise too. You may be pleasantly surprised at how a positive shift in one part of your being begins to affect all others.

As we begin to heal from both feelings of depression and clinical depression, we reduce the symptoms, one being low self-esteem.

Self-Esteem and Confidence

Self-esteem is how we feel about ourselves and our demeanour. One may put themselves down, exhibit destructive behaviour, express self-pity, and not take responsibility for themselves or their lives. This is low self-esteem and once again a learnt behaviour. Fortunately this means it can also be unlearnt!

By making positive choices you can create a positive shift and you can begin by surrounding yourself with supportive people who make you feel good. Take pride in your appearance—look good, feel good... then you'll look even better! Nurture yourself on all levels and give yourself what you need. Slowly and gently take back personal control. Learn to trust yourself as you really connect with the true you, and begin to express yourself with confidence.

Self-love Empowerment

Loving yourself, trusting yourself, and giving yourself what you need strengthens your solar plexus chakra (more on this next chapter). The balance of your solar plexus means your heart will strengthen and you will become empowered—centred in love. This will allow you to also become emotionally independent, with more balance—less over-sensitive and more emotionally intelligent. You'll then open up to all aspects of love and ultimately a more balanced emotional aspect of self.

You may also like to journal your answers to the following questions, for your heart centred connection;

> *What do you love to do, just for yourself, that brings you joy?*
>
> *What song/s or music makes you feel great?*
>
> *What are your favourite pictures, and why are they so?*
>
> *What are your "pleasure" foods?*
>
> *What aromas do you love the most?*
>
> *What is your favourite outfit, and why?*

Occasionally we may take things personally. Rather than doing so—after all it's not always about you—take a step back and see the bigger picture, so to speak. Detach from the emotion and observe the situation, without over analysing. This allows you to shift your balance of focus from the situation to the mind. By looking at things from the combination of both mind and heart, you'll likely find that in most cases the situation will become clearer and you'll feel calmer.

Emotion—e, motion—energy in motion.

This is where I'd like to bring your awareness to how other people's emotions and energies impact on us. Have you ever been feeling fine, then walked into a room and instantly felt the tension between a couple, despite them not saying a word? Were you able to leave and let it go, or did you feel agitated for the remainder of the day?

Or perhaps you've had a certain feeling from entering a party where everyone was happy, dancing and having a great time? Only later you discover that a disagreement has occurred between two of your close friends. You notice that you also start to feel as one of them does? Does this sound familiar? This is picking up on others' emotions. We are like sponges and often if we are not strong within ourselves, we are likely to pick up others' negativity. The more we pick up, the more we need to detach from it and let go of other people's emotions.

Detachment with compassion, one of the most challenging things we can learn to do, is to lovingly detach from someone close—in order to allow him or her to be responsible for their own emotions. This is relevant to all close relationships—parent/child, husband/wife, grandparent/grandchild, and close friends. Detachment with compassion becomes especially challenging if you are empathetic. That means you feel the others' emotions as if they were your own. Discerning whether or not they are your own emotions takes awareness. This usually becomes clearer over time and with personal growth.

Sometimes when we attempt to communicate our emotions with others, it can be misinterpreted and taken by others as a personal attack. In order for effective clear communication, it is important for you to lovingly speak your truth. For example with words like, "I feel ... when you ..." A message delivered this way allows you to not only express your emotions, but also advises others of how their actions affect you emotionally, and perhaps others around them too.

Remember to take a moment and pause before you speak or act in response to an emotionally charged situation. Take a long deep breath if necessary. This will ensure that you are less likely to react, and more likely to respond—creating a better situation for all involved. Learn to make friends with your (less desirable/negative) emotions too, as they often give you messages, and opportunities to learn and grow.

When assistance is offered I suggest you take it, and also ask for assistance when you need it. People generally will not offer, unless they are prepared to assist. If you struggle with accepting offers, perhaps ask yourself, "Why?" You may find you are more concerned for the other person than you are for yourself.

This also works in reverse. You *can* say "no!" when required. This all comes back to valuing yourself and doing so enough by putting yourself first. If you find yourself saying, "I should…", then you can reframe to "I could…"—then you have a choice!

"Should" implies an obligation and may come with feelings of guilt, whereas "could" gives you the chance to choose your action or response. Sometimes we are "emotionally enmeshed" with others in particular situations. We can take things way too personally and to heart at times too. We are always free to choose and this again is an example of when the mind and heart aspects of self intertwine.

When we look at an instance of experiencing the spirit and heart combined, it brings us full circle, back to where we started this chapter—with love. By connecting with who we are—the Divine aspect of ourselves and what brings us joy—we are able to feel a love so deep and profound. You will literally be, "in love"! This is ultimately with yourself and the further you journey into your own healing and growth, the more you'll experience this. You'll grow from living a mostly challenging life to experiencing more of a life in love. Eventually you may even reach a point where you feel this almost always. Some may call it "experiencing heaven on earth", or enlightenment.

In moments of imbalance, ask yourself;

What do I need, right now?

What fills up my cup?

When we don't feel love and joy within our cups are empty and we have nothing left to give. However, when we give to ourselves and fill up our own cup, we have plenty for others. No one gives to us like we give to ourselves. Others will only fill our cups so far. The rest must come from within. By really knowing and loving your higher self you will trust, value, and love yourself enough to give yourself what you need. Please also remember that this is not selfish, it's self first!

For heart balance;

- Allow, acknowledge, accept, express, and release emotions.

- Forgive everyone, including yourself.

- Love and accept yourself, and all others—unconditionally.

- Be empathetic and compassionate.

- Spend quality time with others.

- Laugh often.

CHAPTER 5

SPIRIT

This amazing aspect of self is my favourite area as it is often unacknowledged, unexpressed, and hidden, but lies deep within us all... yes, it is our spirit. It is sometimes referred to as our soul and it is the essence of who we truly are. By connecting with our spirit we are able to really know who we are, and it is through our spirit that we connect energetically with the Divine and all others.

Being spiritual is often confused with being religious. A spiritual person may or may not be religious and a religious person may or may not be spiritual. For example, I myself was christened Anglican but was actually bought up not believing in God at all and certainly did not attend church (unless it was a wedding or funeral). I was bought up an atheist so to speak and I wasn't spiritual either (as far as I knew at the time!). I had snippets of it, but no-one to assist me to nurture the spiritual aspect of myself. I was both fascinated and scared at the same time. However, when I was in my twenties I was strongly drawn to spirituality and of my own accord became a very spiritual person, but I'm still not religious.

I believe in something much larger than ourselves, who I call the Universe or "Divine", (as well as the archangels, angels, ascended masters and other spirits). Religious people also believe in this higher power, but utilise names like God, Allah or Jehovah. My meditation is like my church time, when I both pray (speak to the Divine/spirit) and meditate (listen to the Divine/spirit). Having an image of an old man with a white beard is definitely not my idea of God. I prefer not to use the word God either, for the religious connotations. However, ultimately it's the same... I do believe in a higher power, and my faith and dedication is very strong. You need to make up your own mind for yourself with regards to religion and spirituality.

Having a strong spiritual faith assists me in accepting death as a natural process in the human life cycle—the reality is that we are all born, we live, we pass, and there will be times in our lives when loved ones physically leave us. We go through the grieving/loss process—that may take some time. As I mentioned in the previous chapter, according to Dr. Kubler-Ross we go through the stages of grief; denial and isolation, anger and resentment, bargaining, depression, and finally we become accepting of the reality, of their passing. We can then begin to adjust to life, without their physical presence.

No matter what your faith or religion (or not), it is very important to be gentle with yourself during and after the loss of friends or loved ones. You do this by eating well, getting some gentle exercise, and resting when required. Also by expressing your emotions in healthy ways, and openly and effectively communicating with others. You may also choose to spend some time alone, reflecting upon your thoughts and emotions, and your individual relationship with them as it was on earth, and now with them being in spirit.

Our spirits communicate to us through energy via our "sixth sense" or intuition. Intuition by definition means to understand something instinctively, without a need for conscious reasoning. In-tuition is our inner teacher, our inner teacher is our higher self, and our higher self is our connection to the Divine and Universal collective consciousness. We sense this way through what we know, see, hear, feel, smell, and taste spiritually and energetically.

I'd like to share a story with you. Through one experience I really began to listen to, and act upon my intuition. Despite reading lots about it, and desperately trying to be clairvoyant, it wasn't until I lived it that I truly began to understand. It's *my paint story* and an example of clairaudience that I like to tell others who have difficulty in understanding or trusting their intuition.

During my cancer recovery I engaged in a regular joy activity. That for me at the time was (acrylic) painting. My next project was to paint a flower picture—a gift for a close friend of mine who had assisted me a lot during my treatment. I went off to Bunnings to collect supplies, including a couple of particular coloured paints—that would tie in with the decor of my friend's home. After choosing a neutral coloured swatch I watched whilst the assistant was adding the tint. I heard clearly in my left ear, "You better check the paint!" Of course in my mind I've replied "I don't need to check the paint, I'm watching him put it in there", and didn't give it another thought. So off I went home... and then, when I was all ready to go (paint smock on, canvas prepped), I opened up the pot and was really quite surprised to see that it *was* actually the wrong colour! (It was called Donkey— guess he made an "ass" out of that paint mix!) Feeling rather frustrated at myself that a) I didn't trust my intuition and b) I couldn't get started and actually had to go back again to get the right colour, I stopped for a minute. I realised in that moment that I had actually received a clear intuitive message from spirit. The message was that the paint colour was incorrect. (Then I said to myself... "I *am* clairaudient!"... and really only then, truly believed it!)

This experience taught me a few things;

1) to *go with the first message*/idea/inspiration (rather than second guessing it a number of times—then going with the second one).
2) especially if it was as though you were *spoken to*, "*You* should check the paint", as opposed to "*I* should check the paint", that would indicate your ego thoughts.
3) we are *all* able to receive messages from spirit, if only we are open and receptive.
4) if you have been asking (praying) for guidance, then you're going to get it—so you'd better be ready to receive it! *(Be careful what you wish for because you just might get it!)*
5) always *trust* your intuition!

This is just one story of many that I have in my spiritual journal—where I write down my experiences. Journaling my stories has assisted me to gain validation and trust in the messages I receive as well as my own intuition over the years, further developing the strength of my "clairs"—clairvoyance (clear seeing), clairaudience (clear hearing), clairsentience (clear sensing/feeling), claircognizance (clear knowing), clairgustance (clear tasting) and clairolfactorance/clairalience (clear smelling).

Woah, these are pretty spiritual words and perhaps even a bit woo-woo for some who are still non-intuitive, "five-sensories". However, the truth is that we all receive intuitive messages as we were all born with this innate ability. Some people who are open to spirit may also receive guidance from higher realms of spirit. We don't only hear messages like I did in *my paint story* though. Even non-believers or sceptics receive intuitive messages, just as we all do. Such people don't know where it's coming from exactly, but they are aware that it's there. Someone might say things like he or she's *"got a feeling"*, a particular *"vibe", "something just tells me"*, *"I just* know*" or "I can't explain it, but..."* Yes, that's our intuition and it is sometimes referred also as E.S.P.—extra sensory perception, instinct, insight, inkling, flash, sensitivity or vision. Perhaps you refer to it as another name or have heard it called something else. Regardless, we all have it, but it's a question of whether or not we actually pay attention to it.

Do you trust your higher self—your intuition? Are you open to messages from spirit? Have you ever had a feeling or knew about something even though you couldn't explain how you knew? Have there been times when you've second guessed your "thoughts", only to discover that you would have been better off going with the thought that came to you first?

Again, we are *all* capable of tuning into our sixth sense and receiving messages from our higher selves (also spirit, guardian angels, angels, and the Divine, Universe or God). Connecting and convening with spirit is real. With awareness it is possible for you to tune into your own intuition, if you so choose. Perhaps you could begin your own spiritual or intuition journal to assist you. If and when you learn to fully trust in and act upon the intuition of your higher self, your life will really begin to change, flow, and become more balanced... in a very exciting new way.

So what is the best way to develop our intuition? Meditation. Yes, meditation and thankfully it is not a yogi only practice these days. Many, many people are beginning to open up to, experience, and embrace the benefits of meditation in the Western world. Initially you generally meditate by closing your eyes (temporarily shutting down your physical sight), being in a quiet environment (temporarily shutting down your physical hearing), and quietening your mind (temporarily shutting down your subconscious mind). This opens you up to be receptive to clear intuitive sensing. You may see with your imagination or "minds-eye", sense, know, smell, taste or hear in this space. The more open and trusting you are, the quicker your intuition will develop!

There are many guided meditations available for download to your favourite device. Such audio files are very helpful in the beginning, as are meditation circles and groups. There you may meet others who also share a newfound interest for developing their spiritual selves.

Five Second Meditation

This is a technique I learnt some time ago and have found it so valuable in some tense situations! You can do it anywhere, anytime, and if you choose to be very discreet no one but you will even be aware that you are doing it.

All you need to do is bring your thumbs and forefingers together (this grounds you as it is a physical action) and as you breathe in a long slow breath, say to yourself, "*I am*", then as you slowly and gently breathe out, you say to yourself, "*calm*". Then say to yourself, "*and relaxed*" whilst feeling yourself now being more centred.

That's it! How easy was that? How much calmer did you feel? Imagine using that one when it's really needed! You'll likely find that it gives you just enough space to respond, rather than react.

Spiritual Energy

Everything is made up of energy... everything! Science has proven this. This includes us (as human beings) also being made up of energy and emitting an energetic vibration. We all vibrate our own individual unique energy. It is a sum of our entire being. I call this our personal energy. Our personal energy indicates our physical health, state of mind, emotional status, energetic imprints, and ultimately whether or not we are in a whole, healthy, balanced state.

Depending on our level of intuitiveness we will often be able to pick up on people's personal energy. One of the best examples I can give is of a first time, young pregnant woman and the comment you might often hear, "She's glowing!" Whilst many won't physically see the woman's aura, they will sense it! Others sense this "glow" when a woman is really looking after and nurturing herself and her unborn baby. She's feeling happy, eating well, exercising, and resting when required. She's learning about becoming a mother, and also feeling loving towards and connecting spiritually with the new life inside her.

On the other hand, consider someone is depressed, over or under weight, doing drugs, and surviving on only a few hours of sleep each night. He or she may be inactive, thinking negatively, feeling victimised, and have little mental stimulation. This person is definitely going to emit a totally different personal energy! Now this is not a judgement, but rather a detached, compassionate observation of the truth.

Our personal energy is forever changing, just like our bodies are; with old cells constantly dying off and being replenished with fresh new cells. When we let go of negativity, it makes room for optimism. When we let go of limiting beliefs, it makes way for rational thoughts. In reverse we might choose to eat more healthily, and once we do the consumption of unhealthy foods naturally lessens. If we hold on our energy becomes stale and stagnant. Yet when we let go of the old and welcome the new, we revitalise our energy. Our lifestyles, thoughts, words, attitudes, and actions all contribute to impact on our being and this is evidenced through our personal energy.

As everything and everyone is made up of energy, it allows for us to connect with everyone and everything as well. Take for instance our animals. Some people are attuned to other people's energy, and so too are people often attuned to their pets' energy. Let's look at a dog for example. Many owners are able to tune into their energy to ascertain what he or she needs and what they are thinking and feeling, despite them not being able to speak to communicate it. It's far more than their body language… it's their energy that we are sensing! Many people feel a connection to other things, whether it be plants, animals, sea creatures, people, places or items. What or who do you feel drawn and connected to the most? Do you seem to just "get" the other? Are you aware that you are sensing their spiritual energy?

Energy Systems

The spiritual part of our being contains various energy systems, including the chakra energy system, the meridian energy system, and the auric field.

Our energy systems are closely related to one another and by now you are likely getting the concept that an imbalance in one area directly or indirectly affects all others.

Next we will look more closely at each of our energy systems, as well as how they relate to the five elements of Traditional Chinese Medicine—based on tradition of over two thousand years.

The Chakra Energy System

The sanskrit word "chakra" means "wheel" and the chakras refer to the spinning energy centres of our bodies. There are seven major chakras that I will focus on, and they are related to various areas of our being. Energy sensitive and intuitive people are able to read people's chakras. This can give great insight into any areas of imbalance, in need of healing and repair.

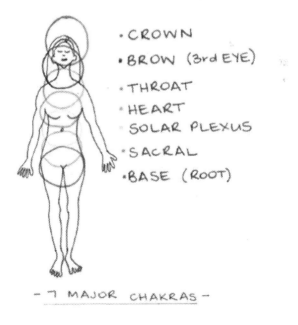

· CROWN

· BROW (3rd EYE)

· THROAT

· HEART

SOLAR PLEXUS

· SACRAL

· BASE (ROOT)

~ 7 MAJOR CHAKRAS ~

The first of the major chakras is the *Base (or Root) Chakra*, located at the base of the spine. This chakra's colour is red and it relates to; material issues, success, grounding, physical body, security, courage, abundance, career, earth energy and connection, and perception of the physical world. Physically it relates to; genitals, legs, feet, spine, male reproductive organs, blood, anus, bones, and adrenals.

The second chakra is the *Sacral Chakra*, located just below the navel. This chakra's colour is orange and it relates to; relationships, sensuality, social life, emotions, female sexuality, indulgence, intuition, pleasure, change, creativity, and movement. Physically it relates to; female reproductive system, bodily fluids, kidneys, and intestines.

The third chakra is the *Solar Plexus Chakra,* located below the sternum (base of the ribcage). This chakra's colour is yellow and relates to; fear, happiness, repressed emotions, worry, intellect, mental activities, self-esteem, personal power, ego, and will. Physically it relates to; digestive system, stomach, pancreas, liver, gall bladder, spleen, adrenals, intestines, skin, metabolism, and muscles.

The fourth chakra is the *Heart Chakra*, located near the physical heart. This chakra's colour is green and relates to; giving and receiving, unconditional love, compassion, empathy, understanding, acceptance, harmony, balance, and forgiveness. Physically it relates to; heart, lungs, arms, hands, breasts, thymus, circulatory system, and immune system.

The fifth chakra is the *Throat Chakra*, located at the base of the throat. This chakra's colour is blue and it relates to; communication, expression, creativity, honesty, reliability, listening, gentleness, and kindness. Physically it relates to; throat, thyroid, jaw, voice, ears, shoulders, speech, mouth, cheeks, weight problems, teeth, and metabolism.

The sixth chakra is the *Third Eye (or Brow) Chakra*, located between the eyebrows. This chakra's colour is indigo blue and it relates to; psychic sight, intuition, perception, inspiration, peace of mind, reasoning, detachment from material possessions, fearlessness of death, and astral travel. Physically it relates to; eyes, sinuses, nose, ears, temples, pineal gland, hypothalamus gland, brain, and nervous system.

The seventh of the major chakras is the *Crown Chakra*, located at the top of the head (where a baby's "soft spot" would be). This chakra's colour is purple and it relates to; hope, faith, bigger picture, connection to everything and everyone, higher power, wisdom, mystical experiences, spiritual purpose, and oneness. Physically it relates to; head, pituitary gland, nervous system, endocrine system, and cerebral cortex (brain).

The health of the chakra energy system mirrors the health and wellbeing of the person.

The Meridian Energy System

Meridians are lines of energy that travel in various pathways throughout the body.

Some holistic health practitioners, like kinesiologists, work with their client's meridian energy to give an individual assessment of a clients being, related to their history and current symptoms. This is done through muscle testing (also called energy testing). Often once the most significant imbalanced meridian is cleared and any necessary lifestyle changes implemented, it creates a "domino effect" leading to healing. Harmony can then be restored throughout not only the meridian and chakra systems, but also the auric field (aura) as well.

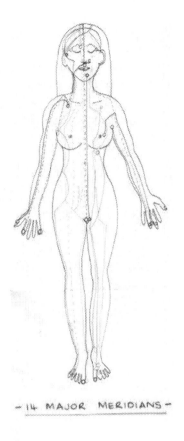

~ 14 MAJOR MERIDIANS ~

There are fourteen major meridians, of the meridian energy system;

Conception (Central) Meridian; runs from the pubic bone, straight up to the chin. It governs the energy flow of the "yin" (feminine) meridians of lung, spleen/pancreas, heart, kidney, circulation-sex, and liver. Associations include; the colours white and of the rainbow, creativity, expression, self-respect, shyness, and dis-eases and disorders of organs and body systems along this meridian line, (including breasts, lungs, immune system, and reproductive system).

Governing Meridian; runs from the tailbone, straight up over the head to the top of the lip. It governs the energy flow of the "yang" (masculine) meridians of large intestines, stomach, small intestines, triple burner, bladder, and gallbladder. Associations include; the colours white and of the rainbow, fear, depression, truth, clarity, support, dis-eases and disorders of organs, and body systems along this meridian line, (including brain, spine, bowel, nervous system, and sinus).

Lung Meridian; begins just below the collarbone and ends at the outer corner of the thumb, on both sides of the body. Associations include; the colour white, grief, sadness, loneliness, vulnerability, boundaries, respiratory system, shoulders, and sinus.

Large Intestine Meridian; begins at the index finger and ends at the opposite nostril, on both sides of the body. Associations include; the colour white, grief, sadness, vulnerable, anxiety, digestive system, and sinus.

Stomach Meridian; begins underneath the eye and ends at the second toe, on both sides of the body. Associations include; the colour red, worry, self-doubt, sympathy, concentration, circulation, digestive system, reproductive system, sinus, throat, and legs.

Spleen(/Pancreas) Meridian; begins at the big toe and ends just below the underarm, on both sides of the body. Associations include; the colour yellow, worry, rejection, lacking confidence, reflection, suppressed emotions, overly sensitive, tension, stress, inability to trust, withdrawal, and immune system.

Heart Meridian; begins at the underarm and ends at the back of the little finger (inside), on both sides of the body. Associations include; the colour red, insecurity, self-doubt, hate, guilt, shock, insomnia, inner joy, arms, circulation, and sleep.

Small Intestine Meridian; begins at the back of the little finger and ends at the opening of the ear, on both sides of the body. Associations include; the colour red, discouraged, internalisation, assertiveness, integrity, lacking self-acceptance, abdominal, digestive system, neck, ears, and throat.

Bladder Meridian; begins at the inner corner of the eye and ends on the outside of the little toe, on both sides of the body. Associations include; the colour blue, fear, anxiety, restlessness, insecure, negativity, overly sensitive, bladder, sinus, urinary system, and spine.

Kidney Meridian; begins on the sole of the foot, below the ball and ends just below the collarbone, on both sides of the body. Associations include; the colour blue, fear, anxiety, insecurity, guilt, nervousness, clarity, workaholic, legs, lower back, immune system, bones, and diaphragm.

Circulation-sex (Pericardium) Meridian; begins at the outside of the nipple and ends at the inside of the middle finger, on both sides of the body. Associations include; the colour red, jealousy, stubbornness, responsibility, communication, grief, circulation, sleep, temperature, and arms.

Triple Burner (Triple Warmer) Meridian; begins on the back of the ring finger and ends at the temple, on both sides of the body. Associations include; the colour red, hopelessness, heaviness, balance, despair, stress, adrenal glands, body temperature, endocrine system, appetite, and head.

Gallbladder Meridian; begins at the outside corner of the eye and ends on the fourth toe, on both sides of the body. Associations include; the colour green, anger, resentment, frustration, rage, low motivation, suppressed emotions, digestion, hips, ribs, shoulders, skin, and gallbladder.

Liver Meridian; begins on the big toe and ends under the breast (in line with nipple), on both sides of the body. Associations include; the colour green, anger, resentment, frustration, bitter, unhappiness, controlling, workaholic, insecure, abdomen, immunity, stomach, wellbeing, muscles, and reproductive system.

Once again, the health of the meridian energy system mirrors the health and wellbeing of the person.

Traditional Chinese Medicine (TCM)—Five Elements

The five elements (fire, earth, air/metal, water and wood) of Traditional Chinese Medicines (TCM), each has corresponding meridians.

Fire – Heart, Small Intestine, Circulation-sex and Triple Burner Meridians. The associated colour is red, root emotion is joy, and the highest expression is love.

Earth – Stomach and Spleen/Pancreas Meridians. The associated colour is yellow, root emotion is reflection, and the highest expression is empathy.

Air/Metal – Lung and Large Intestine Meridians. The associated colour is white, root emotion is grief, and the highest expression is reverence.

Water – Bladder and Kidney Meridians. The associated colour is blue, root emotion is fear, and the highest expression is wisdom.

Wood – Liver and Gallbladder Meridians. The associated colour is green, root emotion is anger, and the highest expression is compassion.

All elements – Governing and Central Meridians.

We have begun to see a pattern emerging within the energy systems, as we also do here with each of the elements directly or indirectly affecting the others. If there is disharmony in one element, they are all directly or indirectly negatively affected, indicated by the – *Ko* cycle. However, if there is harmony in one element, they are all directly or indirectly positively affected too, indicated by the + *Sheng* cycle. I personally believe that when there is disharmony within the five elements, the one to work on correcting first, is fire—it all starts with and therefore, must return to... *love*!

The Auric Field

The Auric Field (or aura) is the energy system surrounding your body and similar to the chakra system, it reflects the person's being. There may be light clear vibrant energy, or dark energy with rips, holes or tears, as well as anything in between. Not everyone is able to sense the aura, but people who have really developed their intuition can.

The aura consists of seven major layers (also called bodies), and are much like the chakra system with its seven chakras. In fact each layer directly relates to each of the chakras. The first layer (associated with the first, base chakra) is closest to the human body and the layers then extend outwards in turn to the outermost seventh layer (associated with the seventh, crown chakra).

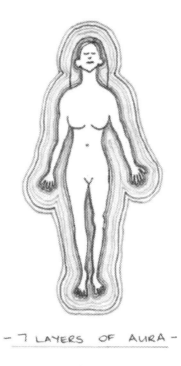

~ 7 LAYERS OF AURA ~

The layers of the auric field are as follows;

The first layer is called *The Etheric Body* and is located closest to the human body. It relates to the state of the physical body's health.

The second layer is called *The Emotional Body* and is the next layer out from the Etheric Body. It relates to the state of a person's emotional health.

The third layer is called *The Mental Body* and is the next layer out from the Emotional Body. It relates to the state of a person's mental health.

The fourth layer is called *The Astral Body* and is the next layer out from the Mental Body. It relates to our connection with other (beings') auras.

The fifth layer is called *The Etheric Template Body* and is the next layer out from the Astral Body. It relates to conscious and unconscious memories.

The sixth layer is called *The Celestial Body* and is the next layer out from the Etheric Template Body. It relates to our connection with unconditional love, intuition and spirit.

The final, seventh layer is called *The Casual Body (or Ketheric Template)* and is the next layer out from the Celestial Body and the farthest from the human body. It relates to our connection and oneness with the Divine/Universe/God.

As with the chakra and meridian energy systems, the health of the auric field also mirrors the health and wellbeing of the person. Generally all of these energy systems will be equally as healthy (or unhealthy) as the others, as they all represent the energetic/spiritual aspect of self.

Following are a couple of examples of imbalances in relation to the mental, emotional, physical, and spiritual aspects of our being;

- Confidence (emotional/mental) or stomach issues (physical) may show up as an imbalance of stomach and/or spleen meridians, earth element, solar plexus chakra, and/or third layer of the aura (spiritual).

- One association of the throat chakra (spiritual) is expression (mental). Therefore, one may present with an imbalance of this chakra if having difficulties speaking (physical) up for ourselves, and expressing the truth of how we feel (emotional). Associations of the throat chakra include the colour sky blue, therefore, we could visualise a soft blue coloured scarf around our neck. Alternatively we could wear aquamarine stone earrings, or carry a blue calcite crystal. This will balance and harmonise this chakra, and also settle any physical throat sensations that may be present.

Testing and healing on an energetic level more often than not reveals the extreme most underlying and significant factors that need addressing. This is not only necessary to ensure optimal health and wellbeing, but also for the very best chance of whole being balance. The spiritual aspect of self simply must be acknowledged, respected for the power it holds, and implemented, for ultimate and transformative healing and personal development.

I hope you've enjoyed this chapter as much as I have writing it for you. There is so much more we could explore with the spiritual part of our being. I could seriously write about it for pages and pages, and I intend to—in a future book! However, at this stage, best we move on to the next chapter. It is a very exciting one as this is where we bring all aspects of our being together, and begin to create some true balance!

> **For spirit balance;**
>
> - *Be your authentic self, always.*
>
> - *Be aware of and trust your own inner wisdom (intuition).*
>
> - *Nurture you, by doing activities you love and enjoy—everyday.*
>
> - *Be self-first and love yourself enough to give yourself what you need.*
>
> - *Connect with nature.*

CHAPTER 6

THE BALANCE OF BEING

Just as achieving and maintaining constant perfection is an illusion, so too is achieving and maintaining constant balance. Pure balance comes from accepting the imbalances, being aware, giving yourself what you need, and doing what is necessary in each moment. This way you return to your **balance point**—that is at the very centre portion of the circles in the image below.

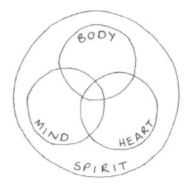

PURE BALANCE
— WHOLE BEING —

The previous chapters have detailed the balance of the individual aspects of our mind, body, heart, and spirit, and you can refer back to them as required for specific healing focus. However, now it's time to bring them all together so that you can be your own solid foundation, to fully support yourself. You'll focus on your own magnificence, embark on seeing the bigger picture, experience health and wellbeing, and really begin to live the life of your dreams!

As I have mentioned, just as every system in our physical bodies effects all others, so too do the different aspects of ourselves. For example, if you haven't done any physical activity for a few days, you may start to feel down emotionally, that may then further escalate into the creation of some negative thoughts. This highlights the effects of one area of imbalance (physical), the impact it can have on the emotional level, and then further onto the mental level. This serves to signify the importance of (whole) being balance. This is imperative for optimal health and wellbeing.

Another example; have you ever come across someone who is highly intuitive, perhaps a psychic, yet he or she takes little care of their physical body and is living a rather unhealthy lifestyle? Or, perhaps someone who is extremely attractive, fit, and healthy in body, yet he or she is also quite unconfident, withdrawn, and shy. Now this is not to draw judgement, but to point out that just because someone is clearly outstanding in one area of their being doesn't necessarily mean that he or she is a balanced being. Our being is like a delicate instrument, if it's finely tuned it will perform at its best. We are all different and within ourselves there can be a variety of different states of being that we can be in, in any given moment.

Depending on the level of balance of your individual being, you may be in a healing phase or a destructive phase. Perhaps you could liken it to a spiral, where you move up and down it, having a balance point in the middle, as pictured below.

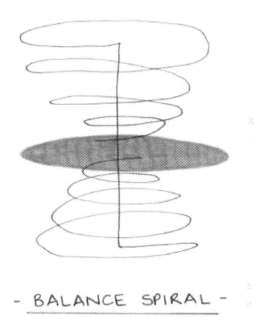

~ BALANCE SPIRAL ~

During the destructive phase you would regress away from health and wellbeing. It can lead to mental issues, lack of faith, negative mindset, and general ill health. If allowed to depreciate further down the spiral mental, physical and emotional exhaustion may be experienced. You could easily develop very unhealthy addictions from this space. A dark cloudy energy builds up in and around you, and it often becomes distinguishable to others. Depression and suicide are also considerations and quite frankly it's not an inviting or welcoming place to be. Some would call this rock bottom!

You will also start to become aware of shifting in reverse however, entering the phase of healing—where you progress towards health and wellbeing. If you consider our physical bodies with the example of a broken bone, it generally takes six weeks or so for us to heal. Likewise, when working on all levels of our being simultaneously, the healing time is often similar but with more life changing and extremely transformative results.

We must be aware of getting too far ahead of ourselves too quickly. If we attempt to race ahead mentally, imbalanced mental issues can easily result. Likewise another example could be gaining a peak balanced and healthy physical condition and then with the adrenaline pumping, pushing ourselves further and further to the extreme. This could possibly lead to exhaustion, adrenal fatigue, and joint issues. We must keep our mind, body, heart, and spirit balanced.

Referring to the balance spiral, you will notice a point in the middle that is the point of balance. Obviously whole being balance is the ultimate, but I'll give you a simple example of an aspect of just one area of being, emotional confidence. Below the balance point we would be unconfident and lack self-esteem. At the point of balance we would be confident, yet humble. Above the balance point we would be over-confident. This means egotistical, over-powered, and even aggressive.

We don't have to get to the absolute top or bottom of the spiral before we go the other way towards balance. At any point along the spiral when we are in a destructive phase, we can become aware and empower ourselves to make the choice to change direction!

Using your newly gained knowledge from within and what you've read so far, you can begin to incorporate whole being balance into your everyday life. Little by little, choice by choice you will start to see positive changes within and around yourself. Love yourself enough to give yourself exactly what you need in each moment and start to live your life, the way you choose to.

Notice that once you make a positive change within one area of your being, it begins to have a profound impact on all other areas. That's when things start to get really exciting for you.

As previously mentioned you may find that keeping a journal and/or diary can be very helpful. Rather than write down everything in detail, just focus on specific areas you feel you need to work on first. This could include what you ate and drank, or what exercise you did and for how long, as you work toward body balance in your physical sphere. Or, it could be keeping a record for awareness of negative thoughts changed to positive affirmations in the mind sphere. Even how you feel and what you wish for, for your spiritual sphere.

Using the activity template below or in your journal, note anything that you'd like to change in this present moment. Then one by one, step by step, adjust your mind, body, heart, and spirit accordingly.

MIND

_____
_____
_____

Action Step 1
Action Step 2
Action Step 3

BODY

_____
_____
_____

Action Step 1
Action Step 2
Action Step 3

HEART

_____
_____
_____

Action Step 1
Action Step 2
Action Step 3

SPIRIT

_____
_____
_____

Action Step 1
Action Step 2
Action Step 3

In times of turbulence, journaling can assist by helping you get back to balance, quickly. It also allows you to view your current situation and monitor your progress over time. It's very rewarding to look back and see the changes and personal growth that you have made in order to regain balance and subsequent wellbeing.

Have you ever been to the doctors with symptoms and had all the relevant tests, only to be told that they were unable to find a physical cause or give you a diagnosis? For example, you accidently fall, and hurt your wrist and forearm. You've had x-rays and bone tests and there are no evident fractures, yet after four weeks you are still in excruciating pain and the doctors just can't explain to you why. We have fantastic medical technologies to rely on today that provide excellent diagnostic tools, yet the professionals don't always provide us with any answers to the cause of dis-ease. Another example that I saw in my practice as a holistic counsellor is those who are trying to fall pregnant and despite time, haven't been successful. This is despite there being no apparent physical reasons, (confirmed through medical testing) why the couple should not conceive a baby. Most Western doctors would not explore the other possible reasons for such symptoms. Instead, sending you home to "give it another try", as well as considering expensive fertility treatments.

However, what if you were to explore the other aspects of self in order to find the blockage or root cause? Sure you are having physical symptoms, but the initial source may have been instigated by other parts of your being; mind, heart or spirit— remembering they are all interlinked and directly or indirectly effect each other.

Please also consider an open-minded perspective on genetics. Is it possible that it's not "in your genes", but perhaps in your ancestral patterns? Learnt behaviour from your family and environment? Subconsciously programmed lifestyle habits? The scientific term epigenetics refers to changes in gene function, occurring without actual changes in the DNA sequence. This is an area of importance, requiring further research. It may well change the way we look at cancer, cardiovascular disease, and other "genetic diseases" in the future.

I have witnessed many clients shift symptoms and dis-eases when viewing and working from a preventative and holistic perspective, effectively cleansing, clearing, and healing on all levels of their being—mind, body, heart, and spirit. You are blessed when you choose to consult with a holistic GP or medically trained professional, getting the best of both worlds!

Now for a closer look at some valuable tools and techniques to assist you in achieving and maintaining whole being balance, that goes beyond healing the individual aspects of your being.

General Rebalance

If you find yourself aware of becoming unbalanced, what you may require is some time and space to lovingly support yourself. This may include;

- **Meditation** and connection with spirit, bringing clarity to the situation.

- **Remembering this** "golden rule" for **work-life balance** when you work for yourself—no matter how much you love what you do, you must honour your (family) responsibilities. When family responsibilities increase, work must decrease!

- **Open communication**—Love yourself enough to put yourself first and give yourself what you needed. Empathetically convey what is necessary to those around you.

- **Rest**—Do what you absolutely needed to do then put your feet up and zone out for a while.

- **Listen to your body's natural body clock** and **follow its signals,** retire to bed when guided. This will prevent any sleep debt and you'll enjoy a restful night sleep, waking refreshed.

- **Cleanse completely** on all levels—mentally, emotionally, physically, and spiritually! Shower, wash your hair, shave, scrub, and cleanse your energy field through visualisation. Re-frame recent negative thoughts through positive affirmations, express emotions, refine your healthy diet, remember who you are, and revise your vision. Then cleanse your environment to; ensure you have a beautiful, clean, and tidy space for you to be in!

- **Connect with** your **higher self and** invoke your **spiritual guides** if that feels right for you. Surrender and ask to be attuned to the highest source of energy—pure divine love—for your strength and protection.

- Do **something** just for you **that brings you joy**—so you feel happy and completely filled—with love, joy and perhaps even euphoria!

- **Become** fully **grounded** for true balance! Put on your shoes and socks—or take them off, enjoy a cup of water or herbal tea, or head off for some (preferably outdoor) exercise.

  The other way to achieve this is to make love or have sex! Yes, our primal creative instincts come to the forefront for a reason, so trust it when the urge arises—just ensure adequate protection if you choose not to pro-create! Sex is grounding, connective (whether with a partner or self), and orgasm releases those lovely feel good hormones.

With time and practice you will *understand your personal energy* so well, especially with the added *awareness* of when you're off-centre. Upon regaining balance on all levels you move back into "the zone"—that space where you feel you're most effective and efficient—for yourself, connecting with others, and in your work.

> How are you feeling right now?
>
> Are you centred, or are you possibly a little off-centre?
>
> Do you feel you are getting to know your own personal energy?
>
> Do you have the awareness of when you are *not* balanced?
>
> Are you becoming more sensitive on all levels?

Perhaps the next time you feel yourself off-balance you might choose to apply some of the techniques I've mentioned above, to regain your personal energy equilibrium!

Allow Surfacing Thoughts and Emotions

Everyone goes through their journey of life with different successes and challenges along the way. Within the light, or shadows of darkness come many opportunities for us to learn, heal, and grow. It's imperative that we travel and be present on our own individual journey, rather than get caught up in our emotions and thoughts—that may surface through comparing ourselves with others.

Thoughts and emotions stem from our conscious and subconscious mind. When we know our own personal energy and balance point so well, we become more aware of when we are off balance. We are sensitive souls and sometimes we find ourselves feeling some pretty intense and crappy emotions.

What we are feeling may be completely relevant to the current situation or event, but we may also be feeling some very old, buried emotions. In the present moment, old emotions may have risen up through the layers to the surface, especially if something doesn't seem right or appropriate in our situation! When this occurs chances are our old emotions are being *triggered* by the present situation or event. That is why it doesn't seem quite right to us. If we truly wish to experience healing and growth, we need to fully allow these surfacing emotions.

We can choose to let it go by putting a lid on it and carry on, sure... but be warned; this choice will ensure that at some other time, these emotions will be triggered and re-triggered again... until we decide to deal with it. That is until *we* decide to heal by diving deeper, to reach the core of our emotions and associated thoughts and actions!

So how exactly can we do that for truly transformational healing, leading to growth, empowerment, and balance?

Take a moment to yourself if possible then and there (the bathroom is always an option—excuse yourself and lock yourself in there if you have to!). Love yourself enough to give yourself the time and space that you need.

Emotional Dissolution

- Let go of thinking about the triggering event or situation. Simply focus on *allowing* the *emotion*...
- Name it...
- Sit with it...
- *Feel* it...
- Ask yourself, "What is my earliest memory of this emotion?"
- Close your eyes, let your mind be spacious, and allow any surfacing images, thoughts or memories. Be aware, but take yourself back to that moment. You may sense that you're in your childhood, emotionally allow yourself to be there.
- Then focus on *feeling* the emotion... (all of it!) This will *not* be nice, but you *will* get through it!
- Be willing to surrender completely! The more you let go and allow, the quicker and more transformative the process.
- You may feel like sobbing, crying, bawling, screaming, yelling—do it! and remember to *breathe*!
- In its own time... it *will* dissolve...
- You may then wish to go one step further by reflecting on the thoughts and memories, to see if you can identify the associated self-limiting belief. This may represent another facet, or layer within a layer, that requires healing too.

As hard as it is, often the best thing we can do is "sit in the crap" of the emotions, regardless of how painful they are, and allow ourselves to *feel* them—in their entirety. Not feeling a little then putting a lid on it... but letting it bubble and splutter as much as it needs to. It can get very intense but eventually, often after many, many tears, it settles down, dissipates, and then finally you feel calm. What is left is *space*... and what is this space then filled up with? *Love*... Pure. Divine. Love... That is pure energy.

The peace, calm, and harmony that emerges after this type of profound emotional healing overshadows the intensity of any pain. This is because you fully allowed it... fully felt it... and fully healed it!

If you are having difficulties accessing your old, deeper emotions then you may find it easier to talk it out with a trusted friend or family member with a compassionate ear. You could also elicit the assistance of a professional therapist too. You'll find a list of useful resources in *Chapter 7—A Little More Help*.

Imagine having the strength, courage and intention to fully manage your emotions. Going through the process above, you'll find you begin to *respond* more—rather than *react* to current situations or events. You may also find you feel a deep love, compassion and forgiveness—for yourself and others.

By recognising your challenging emotional times as opportunities for growth, you'll begin to almost welcome the next wave of surfacing feelings, so that you can clear out more of the old, stagnant "crap" from the past, that holds you back and weighs you down. You'll then travel lighter, feel further emotional freedom, and be more balanced than ever before. As opposed to rough five to ten metre swells, you'll ride the ocean of life that looks more like gentle rolling waves. I wish that for you and if I haven't made my point already... you are worth it, and absolutely deserve it!

Gain Your Highs Healthily

Another situation to be aware of is when you are indulging in habits that aren't necessarily good for you. Yes, I'm talking food, alcohol, drugs, sex, and anything else that elicits a "high" and has you feeling out of control with it. For example, you have been so disciplined about not eating a piece of the cake you made earlier. You make it all the way to the afternoon, and then you decide it's safe. You think "I'll just have one slice"... uh oh... "it's so good, I've got to have more!" You don't seem to have any control. You just know you want... no *need*... *more*.

Okay, *stop* right there! It seems one is too many and ten isn't enough for you, but it's not necessarily the food you are wanting, needing or addicted to. No, what you are actually doing when you are eating the food, or drinking alcohol, or taking drugs or the like... is stimulating the release of those lovely feel good hormones; serotonin, dopamine, oxytocins, and endorphins. That's what you want more of, that is what you feel you need.

Next time you find yourself indulging in a habit or craving something, please don't hurt yourself or others. Be kind and loving to yourself by getting those feel good brain chemicals *naturally*. You have gained awareness through reflective exercises and know the importance of healthily giving yourself whatever it is you need. Engage in your *passions* by doing the things that light you up and make your heart flutter.

Please also be aware that calm, relaxed, and neutral states are good. We don't always need to be on a high, and neither is it sustainable for really extended periods. Calm is good, particularly as calm and centred is where you find your balance point.

Emotional Freedom Technique (EFT) – "Tapping"

Another technique I have often used is Emotional Freedom Technique (EFT) and the results obtained are of profound healing, especially when combined with Louise Hay's physical-metaphysical work!

Sometimes we can be so focused on "being positive" that we suppress what we are *actually* feeling. However, in order to release emotions we must first acknowledge them. EFT allows you to acknowledge, accept, express, and release your emotions. By concluding with a positive affirmation you then re-frame and re-focus on the positive—leaving you feeling emotionally free and mentally optimistic.

When introduced to EFT many Westerners may find that the process of tapping on (the meridian energy lines at) different parts of their face and body, whilst saying things out loud, looks and feels a bit silly. However, it is a wonderful tool for healing on all levels of our being—mentally, emotionally, physically, and spiritually. Below is a basic sequence.

Meridian Tapping – EFT – Emotional Freedom Technique

1. Create a set up statement

    "Even though I feel (name feeling), I deeply and completely love and accept myself"

2. **Rate emotion**/symptom from **0** to **10**

3. Tap karate chop (side of either hand, under little finger joint), thymus (centre of chest) or rub soft/sore spot

(about one inch down and out from inner part of either collarbone), whilst saying set up statement x 3

4. **Tap** with 2 or more fingers on the following with reminder statement (**This (feeling)**) and allow yourself to connect with the emotion/symptom!

    1. **Top of head**
    2. **Inner eyebrows**
    3. **Outside corner eyes**
    4. **Under eye**
    5. **Upper lip**
    6. **Chin**
    7. **K27 (below collarbone)**
    8. **Under breast**
    9. **Under arm**
        Thumb
        Index finger
        Middle finger
        Little finger

5. **Tap "9 gamut tap"** (back of hand, webbing of ring and little fingers) whilst
        Eyes open
        Eyes closed
        Eyes left
        Eyes right
        Eyes clockwise
        Eyes anticlockwise
        Hum
        Count 1-5
        Hum

Take a deep breath in and out, and relax

6. **Repeat tapping** again as per (4 and 5) above with reminder statement (**This (feeling)**)

    Take another deep breath in and out, and relax

7. **Rate emotion**/symptom again, from **0 to 10**

8. If **not 2 or below, repeat** entire process with altered set up statement (**This remaining (feeling)**)

9. If **2 or below, floor to ceiling eye roll** (lock central meridian)

10. Create a **positive affirmation**, repeat **daily** whilst **tapping the 9 points** above, for **21 days**.

* * * * * * *

KISS—**K**eep It **S**imple **S**weetie!

Life doesn't have to be (nor is it meant to be) hard or complicated in any way. Over time, we humans have created it to be that way... So, do yourself a favour and remember to "**K**eep **I**t **S**imple, **S**weetie!"

Simplicity can help to avoid stress caused by busyness and overwhelming situations.

Stress that is either extremely intense or prolonged is harmful to you! It can be helpful to understand what happens as a result of stress and therefore, why it's so important for you to look after yourself, whilst learning to manage *your* stress. If you are sensitive you are likely to be effected by stress more so than others. So, what can you do about it? Plenty!—but it takes a commitment from yourself, to look after *you*!

When we are emotionally stressed, we are likely to be mentally stressed and it will likely affect our physical bodies too. As an example, when we are stressed we may tend to eat. However, when we are really stressed, we may simply have no desire or can't eat at all. Yes, you may be familiar with this sick feeling in your stomach!

You may also be familiar with the sensation of not being able to think clearly when stressed. Stress is our body's reaction to a real or perceived threat/event and the result is that your adrenals go into overdrive—effectively, you are in fight or flight mode. Yes, survival instinct. Your body doesn't know what you are stressed about, for all it knows you are primitive, being chased by a tiger, and you are running for your life!

When in fight or flight mode our bodies shut down the less necessary functions to put all its energy into surviving (responding as if we are being chased by a tiger!). What happens is the front of our brain goes into sleep mode to ensure our energy is directed to more prominent areas such as the muscles, as needed. No wonder we can't think clearly and our stomach feels like it's in knots. Chances are we might have headaches and not be sleeping so well either.

In *Chapter 5—Spirit*, I mentioned the Traditional Chinese Medicine (TCM) and the five elements. The imbalanced emotion worry is associated with the earth element. When stressed this is what most of us do, worry! The organs associated with the earth element are the stomach, spleen, and lymph—part of the immune system. This explains feeling unwell in the stomach and also means that when stressed our immunity is also compromised.

Here are a few techniques for times when you require stress management, that you may find helpful;

- Breathe—take a few long slow, deep breaths.

- Stop and be present (not in the past, not in the future—be in the *now* moment!)

- Breathing combined with stretching exercises like qi gong, yoga and pilates.

- Listen to your body and give yourself what you need. Rest when tired, work when inspired.

- Meditation—by relaxing, you'll give your adrenals a well deserved rest and you will begin to think more clearly.

- Journaling—write down your thoughts and feelings to express them.

- Talk with a trusted family member, friend or colleague—you know what they say, "a problem shared is a problem halved".

- As challenging as it is for some, resist the temptation of reaching for comfort foods—ensure you resist feeding your emotions and choose to nurture your body with nutritious healing foods instead, like fruits, vege, nuts, and seeds.

- Allow others to assist you in healing with complementary therapies such as intuitive massage, reflexology, kinesiology or holistic counselling—to name a few.

Perhaps you also know that feeling you get when you are just so excited or nervous?! Think sporting grand finals or exams...

- adrenalin pumping.
- heart racing.
- sleeplessness and/or (very) early rising.
- racing thoughts.
- fidgeting.
- frequent toilet stops.
- nausea and/or fluttery feelings in the stomach.
- loss of appetite.
- lack of mind clarity.

Although the circumstances may be positive, if your symptoms include all of the above then there's no denying it... you've triggered a state of anxiety and further to intense stress—activating the fight or flight mode!

Unfortunately our bodies don't know the difference between an exciting mental/emotional event like a grand final, or a real life threatening event. Regardless of where it stems from, our body is very responsive and takes action from the signals it's been given! It is not healthy for us to endure intense or prolonged periods of stress, but it *can* be lessened in severity and duration through the various methods of stress management previously mentioned.

In order to regain our balance, as challenging as it may be to have the level of awareness required to acknowledge this, we are to *stop, breathe,* and *relax* as much as possible—especially when we know it will assist us to regain our focus!

Other things you can do that may be helpful include therapies such as acupressure, aromatherapy, emotional freedom technique (EFT) – tapping; sound therapy—music and singing; water therapy—baths; stretching with breathing—yoga); gentle exercise—walking, journaling, and meditation.

Release perfectionism and just *do your best!* Love yourself and give yourself what you need at that time.

Once you relax, you'll find all the symptoms start to resolve and you regain that space required to perform at your very best! Then you can *"go get 'em, Tiger!"*

When you feel stress rising or if it's intense, please also remember that "this too, shall pass" and to keep loving yourself. Also, no one can give you, what you need to give to yourself! If you are so stressed that you think or feel you may harm yourself or another, in any way—*please* speak with someone now, or if needed call Lifeline on **13 11 14** or the associated emergency number in your country.

Perception

Perception is an interesting thing. It is how we view, interpret, and understand things through all our senses. For example, some see household chores as just that, chores. However, it's a part of life and if we shift our view to look at it optimistically, we discover that we are not only creating a beautiful, clean environment to dwell in, but we are also getting some daily activity at the same time!

In every moment we are free to choose. Do you *choose* to shift your perception to cleaning? I suggest you listen to an audio book, podcast or your favourite music to evoke some good vibes as you go about it, and then it won't even feel like you're cleaning... especially if you also consider yourself a "domestic God/dess"! Before you know it you'll be finished. For me personally, cleaning is also a highly intuitive time!

Perhaps you wish to seek help with these home tasks, (enlist the assistance of an earthly domestic God/dess!) but it raises feelings of guilt about paying a cleaner. Someone wise once said to me that when the tasks are left solely up to one person but you pay a cleaner from the household budget, it's like the whole family contributes to the job! Knowing this could be enough to release those emotions, especially when you acknowledge that it keeps someone in a job too. It also buys you precious time to do other things—perhaps even an activity that brings you joy!

Intentions and Goals

You have already gained greater awareness of what your intentions are, throughout the various activities in previous chapters. Intentions (goals) are great motivation to take action. When setting them ensure that they are realistic and achievable.

By breaking big intentions into smaller steps it will make them even easier to accomplish, little by little. After we choose our goals and outline the steps to take, we are to keep our focus, whilst being flexible with them. By following our intuition and taking action we'll be well on our way to achieving those goals!

Energy Clearing

One of your intentions may be to maintain a healthy body. It feels so good to "clear out the cobwebs", and we need to do so regularly on all levels, mentally, emotionally, spiritually, and physically. Did you know that unlike the heart, the lymphatic system doesn't have its own pump? It relies on the muscular-skeletal system (yes, that means movement/exercise!) and the respiratory system (the deeper the breathing the better) to move lymph along—clearing wastes and toxins!

Exercise also helps release feel good hormones that become a natural anti-depressant! This is why activities like qi gong and yoga are so beneficial. You get all the above benefits, plus meditation.

We can allow the result of clearing out the physical to effect the other levels of our being, but if we work on clearing them all simultaneously the results are outstanding! You may like to clear out your mind by reframing self-limiting beliefs and affirming self-supporting ones. Clear the energy of your heart by forgiving those who you need to, including yourself. This will allow space in your heart—that can be filled with peace, love and joy! Taking a swim in the ocean or a walk in the forest (or any other form of nature) regularly, will also keep you clear energetically as well as physically!

How about gardening? Not only do we feel we are nurturing the garden, but also that the garden is nurturing us. What you give out really does return to you multiplied. Next time you're in the garden, take notice of how you feel. You'll likely feel happier, healthier, and more balanced. Take your shoes off and sink your feet into the earth. You may like to sit under some shade for a while too, taking time to admire what you've achieved, and absorbing the cleansing green surrounds. Again we see that all levels of our being are interlinked, as I'm sure you are beginning to truly realise.

Burnout

You can quickly enter a burned out state when responsibilities increase simultaneously with an increased workload. This would mean that you have little time to dedicate to yourself, preventing you from filling your cup. Instead you begin to run on empty. Continuing this way will leave you completely dry, with absolutely nothing to give. Mentally, emotionally, physically, and spiritually it will begin to show, and you then have little choice but to take time out. Stress tends to precede burnout and with those adrenals fired up you'll find yourself mentally cloudy and your output efficiency at a less productive level.

Medical conditions such as chronic fatigue syndrome and experiencing a breakdown can take a long time to recover from. Prevention is better than cure. In order to prevent such a depleted state, we must be aware of when we are "running low on fuel". We are to make conscious choices to balance our time and energy, so as to ensure an adequate efficiency level and clarity of mind.

Make Lists

Lists help us get prepared and organised. Our lives can often be busy and our work perhaps multi-faceted. A list ensures that we prioritise and distribute our time and energy wisely. Remember things may be overlooked if they're not scheduled.

Take your time management a step further by honouring your responsibilities and ensuring you don't put off until tomorrow what can be done today. Leave time and space to allow for the "curve balls" that may present in your day and communicate effectively with any other parties involved. No more excuses, or shifting the blame or responsibility to others (unless you are efficiently delegating). Prioritise, be accountable, and follow through...basically get it done!

Play

It can't be all work though, and therefore, it's so important for us to include regular play and fun into our lives too—particularly as adults! As we grow older, we often have more responsibilities and can be quite serious at times, especially if we have young people reliant on us and who are a regular part of our lives.

The children in our lives know how to have fun, and do so regularly. Yet as mature adults we sometimes need to put in a little more effort to be playful and nurture our "inner child". It relaxes us, relieves stress, and stimulates the release of feel good hormones—that ultimately is a form of self-love, nurture, and self-healing. Some join in and play with the children, even letting themselves get dirty and make a mess. Others play sport, listen to music while dancing or get creative with painting, drawing or cooking. There are so many ways to play and have fun, and it's unlimited by the use of our imaginations!

Let Yourself Be Seen

When we wear clothes that suit us and we are comfortable in what we wear we feel confident, and it's that confidence that is the key to being gorgeous. Despite what we wear, when we are confident it allows our spirit to shine through and guaranteed we will not be the only person who notices this. Think about it, we have (or seen others who) looked amazing, yet aren't confident and it shows. Then there are other times when we aren't wearing anything special yet seem to glow with inner beauty and confidence!

Let yourself express who you truly are (and if you like let your creativity run free). Do this through what you wear, how you walk, how you speak, and how you interact with others. Shine with confidence as you express your personal energy.

However, we must be aware of the possible ego trap! If we allow our ego (through our unhealed subconscious mind) to dominate, and disregard our heart and spirit, it can often lead to an imbalanced state. This would mean the ego predominantly leads us in our thoughts, words, and actions. The ego distances us from who we truly are and can have detrimental effects on our health and wellbeing if not tamed! Yet, when we choose to make decisions weighted evenly between conscious mind, heart, and spirit, this allows us to be rational, realistic, and self-reliant. The results of those decisions are more balanced and aligned with our true self.

Love Yourself Enough To Give Yourself What **You** Need

What do you need?

Perhaps it might be one of the following, that has been discussed previously and calls for repeating.

- take *time out* to rest and recharge.
- ignite the flame of *passion* within you, and *engage in your passions regularly*.
- do more or varied *exercise*.
- *value your opinion of self* greater than anyone else's.
- *not be influenced by* the unhealthy habits of *others*.

- *reduce* your daily *food treats*—to weekly.
- eat *smaller portions* of foods, that you know you could do.
- *eat more healthily* in general.
- express your *creativity*—cook, paint, sew, draw, sing, dance or garden.

Taking time out from our roles and routines allows us to connect with our inner being and then express our authentic selves. Room is made for self-discovery, healing, growth, and empowerment. This can be quite profound, especially when no expectations are set and we are open and receptive to trusting ourselves and the experience.

Whether you purchase a retreat package or simply take some time out, away from home, work, family, and your everyday life, retreating allows you to connect deeply with your true self. It could be for one day or a week. It could be to a place nestled in nature or somewhere a little busier, yet where you feel completely relaxed. You may already be on your healing journey and know what you need from your retreat, or perhaps you choose to have a set program, being guided, and assisted by others. By setting your intentions before or early on in your retreat, you will open yourself up to amazing possibilities.

Yearly retreating is a valuable, self-loving, and self-first activity that is beneficial in so many ways for every adult human being. Most people take yearly holidays with others, and we may get snippets, but do we really connect deeply with *our own* spirits, connecting with and fully expressing our authentic selves? Are we still in our regular roles of everyday life? Think about how much work we generally do whilst on family holidays... there is a lot of giving to others, and perhaps just a little to ourselves. This is why on top of the family holiday many of us also choose to go on a couples retreat, boys fishing trip, girls shopping weekend or group outing—and feel so good for it! Retreating allows us to fully relax, rebalance, energise, and revitalise on all levels— mentally, physically, emotionally, and spiritually. We shine as our whole being illuminates, with light and love.

Gratitude

Regularly express gratitude for all the blessings that you have in your life. Often things and people get overlooked, yet we all deserve to be acknowledged and appreciated. The more you give thanks for these blessings the lighter your being, the better you will feel, and the more the Universe will bestow unto you!

Be Open to Possibilities

Ah, the big wide expanse, open and full of infinite possibilities... are you open to them? A closed mind is an inflexible one, but with a flexible mind we are able to transcend to places we've never been.

Sometimes we are given amazing opportunities. Step forward and centre. Be big. Be brave. Be bold. Get out of your comfort zone and trust yourself to try something new. You never know, you might actually enjoy it!

Now that you are opening up to your spiritual side, there are many avenues for exploration. Dive deeper into what interests you—angels, ascended masters, and other planes of existence. Meditation, channelling, and energy healing. Perhaps you're more science based and prefer to devour things from that perspective. Regardless... go on, give yourself permission and explore the possibilities! There's always more we can learn, experience, and understand.

Quality v Quantity

When we choose more, we are choosing quantity. However, what if we aimed for gaining *quality* with everything, including time and energy, *over quantity*? For example, it could mean ten minutes on the phone with your mother, really connecting. This soon becomes more treasured than the multiple hours you spent with her just making up time, or because you felt you had to. Another example is the big "slapped together" meal that leaves you feeling full and heavy. How much more quality would there be if you choose a small, nutritious meal—that was lovingly prepared.

It's our choice to choose quality over quantity. If we incorporate quality into our very being and everyday life, we will find that we live a rich, rewarding existence.

Older Doesn't Necessarily Mean Wiser

Have you noticed how children these days are super switched-on? We may have years of earthly experience on them, but gee the younger generation have knowledge and skills that we can learn from. In fact, if we are aware, everyone and everything around us has something to teach us, no matter what our age. That is, *if* we are prepared to get out of our own way, be neutral in our perceptions, and open to the possibilities!

Patience

With clear vision often comes a need to have it yesterday. However, we aren't there yet and the world (and the Universe!) doesn't work that way—despite us wishing at times that it would. We simply can't wave a magic wand and instantly have many of the things and situations that we want, unless it was meant to be that way.

Once we have set our intentions, we are to *let go* of the desired outcome and simply take positive, inspired action in each present moment. It is through the present that the future pathway is paved. Plus, it's often not about the destination... but about the journey. Keeping your target in the back of your mind and enjoying the process will make the achievement all the sweeter when you eventually get there! Plus, then you'll actually be happy all the way there.

Be aware of the comparison trap! Think the content tortoise rather than the frantic hare, and remember to travel your own unique journey.

Find Your Passion and Purpose

What do you love? What do you love to do so much that when you engage in it, and the hours often pass, you lose all sense of time? (This is because you are so present and in the moment with it). What fires you up inside, like nothing else? This is your *passion*. This is your *purpose*.

Many people in the world affect their environments through greed for money, ego based perceptions, and stale, disharmonious, toxic energy. Whether your passion and purpose is your work or your hobby is irrelevant. What's relevant is that you actively engage in it, in some shape or form! It feeds you. It sustains you. The world needs "balanced" people in all fields, now more than ever. Whether your passion is land conservation, energy healing or telemarketing it doesn't matter. The world needs you to be passionate!

We begin where we are, right now and once we find our balance point, it really is time to step out of the shadows and immerse ourselves into our chosen passionate field. In doing this we are fulfilled and can positively influence others. Not by doing anything specifically, but simply by *being* ourselves! It doesn't go unnoticed. People see you radiate your light, and it inspires them.

You do not necessarily have to be consciously aware of it (though you may be), but your clear, balanced energy of being resonates at such a high frequency that others are automatically positively influenced by you. This is the law of resonance. Therefore, you may find new people entering your life as you begin attracting and meeting more like-minded people.

Personal and True Empowerment

Balanced power doesn't come from being bossy, controlling or aggressive. Dominating others is an imbalance of power. Being dominated by others is an imbalance of power also. When we are quite sensitive and compassionate we often lack strength and give away our power to others, to the detriment of our own needs. We sense their impending unhappiness or dissatisfaction, and give in to them in order to keep the peace. This is related to the sacral, solar plexus, heart, and throat chakras. This can lead to depleted energy. Therefore, ensure you take time out for self and focus on your own loving heart, filling yourself up. This is imperative in order to retain your personal strength, and so you may continue to give to others.

You are so much more powerful than you know. Embrace your own inner strength. Step into it. Own it. The only way others can take our power is if we let them have it! The same goes for others affecting us. They can only affect us, again, *if we* let them.

Choose to embrace your personal power, centred in love. This strength of the solar plexus chakra provides confidence, self-esteem, and strength, supporting the balance of the heart chakra. Remain compassionate towards others and considerate of their needs, but also speak up for yourself about your own. Express your truth and act with integrity. This is what true love-based empowerment is. Be the most magnificent being that you know you can be... that you are!

Personal Commitment

Whether you eventually choose to actively commit to serving our world is up to you. However, what is paramount for your own healing, growth, and empowerment journey is that you begin with committing to yourself. The thing is that no one else can do this for you. Personal commitment begins and ends with *you*. *You* are the one who needs to choose *your* own commitment to self.

Once you've done this you can then act upon your commitment. Through positive choices and experience we really learn and grow, as we incorporate new ways of being and living into our everyday. Choices plus actions always equals consequences. However...

Positive Choice + Positive Action = Positive Transformation!

You make the positive choice. You take the positive action (guided by your higher self). Then just like a butterfly emerging from its cocoon, you witness your own transformation—right before your eyes.

Balance Point

Pure balance is the balance point where we are harmoniously aligned in mind, body, heart, and spirit. We are human and therefore, we all continue to experience new things as we grow; lessons, events, and stages of life. To expect to live in a state of pure balance every moment of every day, day after day, is an illusion and concept of mind that only leads to disappointment.

It's like striving for perfection in everything you do, yet only feeling satisfied when you achieve it one hundred percent. Just as the perfection is in the imperfection, so too is the balance in the imbalance.

We must therefore, learn to flow and adapt to our circumstances and experiences. That will allow us to feel more at ease within ourselves and our lives. Those who are extremely sensitive, "control freaks", and perfectionists, often have the biggest challenge ahead of them.

However, it is not only do-able... it will change you and your life, in the most extraordinary ways. Life will eventually become more fluent.

You'll experience times in the space of your balance point, and times when you are not. Therefore, we need to understand the message of the imbalance as it arises. We may start off looking and feeling as if our life is a rollercoaster. Yet with some time for change, new tools, and positive action, it can transform to be more of a gentle wave that you ride along your journey.

Like perfection and control, for balance we must learn from the ebbs, let go of what we can't control, and focus upon what we can—flowing with the natural waves of life. We are to be the best version of our true selves, with the knowledge, skills, and tools we have at each moment. We can then experience our own optimal state of health and wellbeing.

Remember;

The answers lie within,
as you surrender and
flow in the grace of your spirit.

Live in the present moment and
create the life you choose to live.

Be in harmony with your environment,
the earth, and
Universal cycles.

Live by Divine Time.

Lead by example.

Concentrate on what IS actually in your control.

KISS—keep it simple sweetie.

Breathe.

Trust in yourself.

Live in truth and integrity.

Lovingly express your truth.

Share through experience.

Live intuitively.

Keep your personal energy clear.

Regain your balance.

Shine.

FOR WHOLE BEING BALANCE;

MIND—*Be positive and optimistic, yet realistic. Engage in mind stimulating activities that you like. Awareness. Review and re-assess your life regularly. Dream. Connect with your inner wisdom. Meditate. Work/create when inspired. Heal self-limiting beliefs from the subconscious.*

BODY—*Eat wholesome natural foods. Drink pure clean water. Awareness. Get a little sun and breathe fresh air into your lungs. Exercise regularly. Take some time to rest and relax.*

HEART—*Allow, acknowledge, accept, express, and release emotions. Spend quality time with others. Awareness. Forgive when necessary. Laugh. Be empathetic and compassionate. Love and accept yourself and others, unconditionally.*

SPIRIT—*Do activities you love and enjoy, everyday. Connect with nature. Awareness. Be your authentic self. Give yourself what you need. Be self-first. Nurture you. Listen to and trust your intuition.*

CHAPTER 7

A LITTLE MORE HELP

If you are having trouble letting things go, being present, find you are too far into the future or simply feel like you just need a little more help, please don't think you have to get through things alone. There are always many wonderful people and modalities that can assist you!

If you are comfortable with complementary therapies, then you could try the ancient art of reflexology. It is like a foot massage and assists the body's own natural healing abilities. It is a holistic therapy. That means it treats you as a whole... your mind, body, heart, and spirit. It releases any blockages and allows your energies to be balanced and flowing. The Reflexology Association of Australia has further information and a list of registered practitioners on its website, listed with other recommended websites at the end of this chapter. Other complementary healing modalities that may be of assistance to you are listed below.

CLARE EVANS

Healing Modalities

These include; acupressure, acupuncture, aromatherapy, ayurveda, colonic hydrotherapy, cranio-sacral therapy, energy healing, holistic counselling, hypnotherapy, intuitive therapy, kinesiology, massage therapy, meditation, myotherapy, naturopathy, neuro-linguistic programming (NLP), osteopathy, pilates, qi gong, reiki, shiatsu, traditional chinese medicine, and yoga.

If you'd prefer a more conventional style of therapy, then counselling or psychology may be the way to go. The practitioner will assist you to go within, to let go or discover the answers, for yourself. You don't have to be clinically depressed before you seek help of such a practitioner either! Other practitioners that may be of assistance are; chiropractor, dietician, medical practitioner or personal trainer. Go where you feel drawn to.

Please be aware that as in all professions, just because someone works in a specific field, doesn't always mean he or she is competent at or compassionate in their job. Some will be highly qualified and have years of experience, yet fail to come across as friendly or empathetic. Some may not even appear to embrace or enjoy their chosen field. There are also many unqualified therapists out there who are very, very good at what they do—and could be your friend or neighbour! Communicate with others; someone you know may well have had excellent results within a certain therapy. However, what works for one doesn't necessarily work for another, as we are all individuals with individual preferences and responses. Allow your intuition to guide you. If it feels right for you to go to a certain therapist, trust it.

No time or money for therapy? ... Believe me, *you are worth it!* If you want to instil change and bring balance into your life, put yourself as priority number one, above all else and all others. Let yourself be self-first (it's absolutely *not* selfish) and take care of you, on all levels. Forgo some of your other unnecessary expenses or obligations and nurture your mind, your body, your heart, and your spirit—to feel whole again. Only you can truly value you and make the decision to give to yourself.

There are other less expensive options available to you too, but some take time. Books are an excellent resource for self-help, motivation, and inspiration. It's important to find books that are significant and of interest to you! Browse your local library, bookstore or online and see what appeals to your unique spirit. Trust that your inner wisdom will lead you to the right book for you, at exactly the right time. However, the following three recommended books are all available through *Hay House* and *Hay House Australia* and may also be in the self-help/spiritual section of your local bookstore or library.

A beautiful gift to yourself or others who are going through a challenging time health wise is the best seller, Louise Hay's *You Can Heal Your Life*.* No doubt you've heard about this life transforming book already, as millions of copies have been sold world-wide. This book will inform you about the power of affirmations and the mind-body connection.

Sonia Choquette's work is powerful, yet simple. Her books are easy to read and she has a beautiful one called, *The Answer Is Simple... Love Yourself, Live Your Spirit*. It will assist you to leave your ego behind and love yourself, through connecting with your spirit.

If you are after a gentle introduction to your connection with the beautiful angels, you may like to read Doreen Virtue's *Healing With The Angels*. Doreen has written many books about angels and this one will soon have you working with these magnificent beings in healing yourself and all areas of your life.

When we re-read transformational books such as these we usually find ourselves healing and growing more each time. We generally get something different from them each time they are read, and the reason is because we are at a different place along our journey.

Some additional reading suggestions for further assistance and inspiration are listed below.

Books

- *A Return To Love* – Marianne Williamson
- *Crazy Sexy Cancer Tips* – Kris Carr
- *Dying To Be Me* – Anita Moorjani
- *Heal Your Body* – Louise L. Hay*
- *Healing With The Angels* – Doreen Virtue
- *Heaven And Earth* – James Van Praagh
- *I Can See Clearly Now* – Dr Wayne W. Dyer
- *Live Your Best Life* – Dr Lily Tomas and Greg de Jong
- *Lovability* – Dr Robert Holden
- *Love Is The Message* – Paula Armstrong
- *Many Lives, Many Masters* – Dr Brian L. Weiss
- *Money A Love Story* – Kate Northrup
- *The Answer Is Simple… Love Yourself, Live Your Spirit!* – Sonia Choquette
- *The Barometer Of Your Soul* – Annette Noontil*
- *The Biology Of Belief* – Bruce H. Lipton, Ph D
- *The Highly Sensitive Person* – Elaine Aron
- *The Secret Language Of Your Body* – Inna Segal*
- *The Seeds Of Transformation* – Maggie Erotokritou
- *The Survival Of The Soul* – Lisa Williams

- *The Tapping Solution* – Nick Ortner
- *Trust Your Vibes* – Sonia Choquette
- *You Can Heal Your Life* – Louise L. Hay

* References for causes of physical symptoms/ailments.

Diet related books

- *Additive Alert* – Julie Eady
- *Eat To Live* – Dr Joel Fuhrman
- *Green For Life* – Victoria Boutenko
- *Super Immunity* – Dr Joel Fuhrman
- *The Amazing Liver Gallbladder Flush* – Andreas Moritz
- *The Mucusless Diet Healing System* – Prof. Arnold Ehret

Websites

- www.brucelipton.com – Dr Bruce H. Lipton
- www.clareevans.com.au – Clare Evans
- www.drfuhrman.com – Dr Joel Fuhrman
- www.druyoga.com – Dru Yoga
- www.drwaynedyer.com – Dr Wayne W. Dyer
- www.empowertotalhealth.com.au – Empower Total Health
- www.hayhouse.com – Hay House
- www.kriscarr.com – Kris Carr
- www.naturaltherapypages.com.au – Natural Therapy Pages Australia
- www.reflexology.org.au – Reflexology Association of Australia
- www.thetappingsolution.com – Nick Ortner

CHAPTER 8

BEYOND SELF...

By now you have likely implemented some subtle changes within yourself and your life, or you may have changed a lot. The important thing though is that you *have* made positive changes towards bringing yourself back into balance and being true to yourself.

Now that you are aware of the simplicity of living a life of pure balance, it's time to share your knowledge and love with others, through your relationships, as well as the world around you.

Relationships

It is said that others enter our lives for a reason, a season or a lifetime. Some may love and support us always, and some come to teach us a valuable lesson that we need to learn. Others may be with us for intense or extended periods of time and we may connect strongly during our relationship with them, but it may not necessarily be for always. Relationships can be easy at times, and they can be complicated at others. Trust yourself when you know a relationship is developing, and also if and when it's time to let it go, even if you've known them for your entire life. This allows you both to move on with your individual journeys. As you heal and grow, so too will many of your relationships. Surround yourself with loving and supportive people as much as you can.

In balance you may well find that others will magnetise themselves to you as you emit a radiance of health, love, joy, and happiness. Embrace this and share your shining light with the world...

Partnerships

Do you have current partner relationship challenges? Perhaps you feel like the two of you are moving in separate directions, or even as if you've outgrown the relationship somewhat. You may even be thinking it's all but over.

It doesn't have to mean that you will, should or have to separate if you don't want to though! If one partner heals and grows quicker than the other, he or she also has the opportunity to teach their partner much of what they've learnt.

Do you still love each other and connect on a soul level? When was the last time you went on a date, just the two of you? Someone once said to me, *"Babysitters are designed to save rocky marriages!"* Are you able to come back to that loving, connective energy, allowing the two of you to grow stronger in love?

Almost all relationships have their challenges at times. Throughout more than eighteen years of marriage to my darling husband, what I've learnt is that it's important for the two partners to *support each other in being their true selves.* Each is to be equal and allow each other to live their own separate lives, but *share* them, together in love.

You could look at it a bit like a double yoke in an eggshell—each are equal and separate, but together! As long as you give each other the space to be and do, and enjoy *quality,* loving time together, a harmonious partnership is able to be maintained and likely strengthened. Also, it's great to come together and openly discuss "your world" and "their world", and see the light of passion in their eyes (and for them in yours) as you converse. Ensure you give your partner the respect he or she deserves and remember to listen, wholeheartedly.

Do you seek guidance from others, regarding your relationship? I said a very long time ago, *"The only two people that can truly know and assess a relationship, are the two that are in it!"* The opinions that others (including psychics) give you are a snapshot in time as *they* perceive things to be—from an outside perspective. Mind you at times this can also be enlightening! *You* hold the power! It is up to you and what *you* feel you need to do.

Is your partner open to the "new and improved" you? Or, if you are going through a difficult time personally is he or she supportive and allows you the space you need? Are you supportive and allow him or her the space that *they* need? How does your partner feel about your relationship at present? Endings are opportunities for new beginnings. Perhaps it could mean the *beginning* of a new stage in your relationship?!

We are to be very supportive of healing and growing in relationships, unless there is an undeniable, definite means for separation—like abuse for example. However, it's your life. Please don't make decisions based on what *anyone* else says. You, and *only you* (and your partner) can decide on your future!

CLARE EVANS

Open, effective communication with your partner is imperative, moving forward.

Sit in quiet contemplation. Give yourself some time and space *(as much as you need!)* at this point to ask yourself the question; What does your entire being—body, mind, heart, and soul truly say about your relationship in the present, and what it may hold for the future? Then surrender and listen deeply, for the honest answer... Plus, a healthy partnership will set up a good solid foundation for raising happy and healthy children.

Children

The earlier you start with raising healthy balanced children, the better. The older they are, the more habitual their life becomes (from subconscious brain programming by about six years of age, remember). Children then may be more resistant to changes, especially if allowing themselves to be influenced by others and mirror what their peers are doing. Again communication is paramount to all healthy relationships. Talk to them, listen and get to know your children better. Get creative with them, and let your hair down a little too.

We, as parents are our some of our children's greatest teachers (as our children are ours also). We don't always get it right, but we generally strive to do the best we can—with the knowledge, skills, and tools we have at the time. Please remember this and like your school teachers may have said to you in the past, "Give yourself a pat on the back"!

Role Model Reflection

Are you a good role model for your children?

After all, we all would like to have happy and healthy children!

Do you exercise daily?

Eat healthy foods and beverages?

Do as you say?

Communicate openly?

Take time out for yourself?

Have a positive mindset?

Acknowledge, accept, express and release emotions in safe ways?

Are you a good listener?

Speak calmly and clearly to others?

Rest when tired and work when inspired?

Spend quality time with them?

Are there any changes you wish to make, in order to lead an even better example for them?

What can *you* learn, from them?

If we take the time to connect with the children in our lives, they often have gifts to share with us and can assist us to re-connect with our own inner child. Spend some quality time with them, let go and have a little fun!

When you are used to having a lot of (quiet) time to yourself in your home, it can take a little adjusting to having children in your presence, 24/7! Strangely enough though, when the children go back home or to school, that can also take some adjusting to too (yes, to that stillness... and sweet silence... ahhh...).

Here are a few of my favourite strategies that have assisted me over the years that you may also find beneficial;

- Remain motivated and use your time wisely, perhaps by making a list of what you want to achieve each day or week, and work through your prioritised list.

- Consider doing a swap with a friend; you have their children for an hour or two—or a day, then have them mind yours another time. This especially works well if you need some time out of the home—I'm thinking Christmas shopping, but some may prefer time to self for more indulgent treats!

- To prevent (your children's) boredom, schedule activities and tasks for the mornings and more quiet time to selves (like reading, listening to music (headphones!), drawing or journaling) in the afternoons—this includes Mum or Dad too!

- Give children age appropriate tasks. Teach them about what is involved in taking care of and running your home. This gives "home schooling" a whole new perspective—you are teaching them valuable life skills!

- Ensure children go to bed by an agreed time, even if they don't go to sleep straight away (perhaps reading for a while). This gives Mum (and Dad) valuable time to unwind (and be together) at the end of the day. Children need and benefit from having set boundaries.

- Relax and go with the flow... it doesn't matter if the living room is untidy, or there's a loud, consistent beat coming from your teenagers room! Half an hour or so before dinner should be enough time to have a "team effort" tidy-up! Besides... before you know it your children will be all grown up, left home, and you'll be wishing there was a mess or loud music playing. It's all about being present, and enjoying the moment.

Close Relationships

When you encounter negativity within or from others, take a step back into your heart and gain a greater view of the situation. Ask yourself what this is about and what you need to do, if anything. Then trust the intuitive answers you get.

We can also only assist others in our lives as much as they are prepared to help themselves. Otherwise, it tends to be very taxing on our energy. Assert healthy boundaries and lovingly reflect back to others their own mental and emotional "stuff". When they are ready assist them to make improvements first, rather than massive changes, and let them know you are there to support them. Encourage them to make gradual, healthier choices in their life, one step at a time! By letting go and releasing the old, we make room for the new.

When you have an issue with someone my suggestion is to first take it up with him or her directly and personally, through open communication. Find out both sides of the story, seek the truth, detach emotionally, and see things from a higher perspective. Once you name someone publicly it becomes an open personal attack. To "advertise it" can be potentially damaging, especially when the person being blamed or judged hasn't had a chance to explain his or her side of the story. It's important for all parties involved to work together towards a win-win solution wherever possible. Quite often people are too quick to judge and attack others. Expressing your emotions is healthy and necessary for healing, as long as it is done in healthy ways.

Each person in our lives can be a reflection for you, giving you a glimpse of who you are if only you'll take a look. When you encounter someone who irritates you in some way, allow him or her to be a *mirror for you*. What is it about him or her exactly, that is irritating you? This is likely what you don't like about yourself, or what you don't (or wouldn't) choose for yourself. For example, let's say that someone around you is being very loud. He or she may be annoying you because you are quiet by nature and prefer a calm environment. This highlights what you don't like about yourself—being loud and what you do prefer and choose for yourself—quiet and calm. Another example is someone is really confident—over confident and perhaps a little egotistical. He or she may be annoying you because you have low self-esteem and couldn't imagine yourself being so boisterous. This highlights what you don't have, yet may wish to have more of; confidence in yourself. It could also mean that although you'd like to improve your self-esteem, you wouldn't wish to be *that* confident, preferring to be more balanced in your personal power.

Being alert to and allowing others to be your mirror will be a valuable tool in getting to know yourself. Doreen Virtue, PhD taught me a good releasing technique when you allow someone to "push your buttons", raising thoughts and emotions by stating;

"I lovingly release that part of me that irritates me, when I think of you."

When someone close to you has made a choice in their life it can sometimes indirectly impact you and your life. If you find it challenging to see his or her point of view or understand their choice, it can be absorbing and you may be tempted to do anything and everything you can to help—even attempt to get them to change their mind...

Rather than taking on the issues of others we must learn to detach, and respect and accept the choices others make in their lives. After all, we all have different lessons to learn!

It's also important to acknowledge, accept, and express your own emotions with regards to how their decision has impacted upon you. Keep the loving lines of communication open and be there for them when they need you for support too.

If you are someone like me—very independent and gives constantly to others—it's imperative that you also give to yourself and allow yourself to receive! Accepting offers and gifts from others and taking time out to do things you enjoy not only fills your heart up, but it does so to overflowing—ensuring you have more than enough to give to others!

We aren't to change anyone else, but instead we are to accept them for who they are. You may also like to affirm; *"I deeply and completely love and accept myself and all others"*, whilst sending them love. Therefore, the next time someone gets under your skin, rather than getting stuck in the emotion of annoyance or frustration, detach from it and view from a higher perspective. This way you may see what's really irritating you. Take a look in the mirror and release that part of yourself that irritates you.

On a brighter note, you might also begin to be aware of when someone is being a mirror that makes you feel good! What do you like about a particular person or his or her behaviour? This is likely a reflection of what you like about yourself or what you do (or would) choose for yourself. What is reflected back to you resonates, because it's in line with your spirit. For example, you see an average person walking along the street with absolute unmistakable confidence. He or she is bright, happy, and definitely catches your eye with their glowing aura (that you may or may not consciously be able to see/sense). You admire them as they are mirroring for you how you feel when you are that confident, or what it would be like to be that confident. You may find that some of that lovely energy "rubs off on you" (collecting it in your aura) and all of a sudden you feel pretty confident too—and begin to strut your stuff down the street!

That's how we can be positively influenced by people we've never even met. Imagine the "hundredth monkey effect" if everyone is connected with their true selves, balanced, and loving. Their energy would positively influence others, creating a snowball of love right across the room, house, street, suburb, city, state, nation... the globe! We *can* create an absolutely wonderful world. I'm ready and I hope you are too.

Social/Community

We as humans are social beings. As you have already read, every single interaction we have with those who are outside ourselves has an impact on our being. By ensuring we are balanced and healthy, we put ourselves in the best position to live and interact harmoniously with others.

Naturally we are social with those who are in our immediate circles; family, friends, and colleagues. But what about further outside those circles? You have already ascertained what activities you love whilst reading this book. By being social and engaging in the relevant community, you extend and share your joy further—with others. Besides, your family, colleagues, and perhaps some of your regular friends may not be at all interested in the same things you are passionate about. Be true to you. Go to where you are personally drawn to, like a honey-bee to the hive. Fill yourself up!

Whether it be a sporting club, charity or hobby group, ensure you make the time to connect with like-minded souls regularly—especially as these are the people who share your passions. It will lift everyone's spirit and fill your heart with even more joy. Plus, you may very well make new, lifelong friends in the process. Now that's worth getting out of your comfort-zone for!

Career/Financial

Are you working in a field that truly suits you, and does it support you financially? Or, perhaps you dream of a new career, money being a lesser consideration from the satisfaction you know you'd get out of it?

We spend so much of our days at work. Therefore, how we think and feel about it is going to have a significant effect on our health and wellbeing. Some of us choose our passions as our careers, and others may choose to transform educational training into a career and passion into a hobby.

Even if we enjoy our job though there are instances when it's overshadowed by challenges bought forth from others in our work environment, often creating an energetically toxic work space. You may choose to undergo some personal healing and growth to be able to co-exist with others and thrive in such an environment. Or, you may also choose to continue your job, just at another place of employment. We are always free to choose, and hopefully this choice will provide a more suitable atmosphere for you to spend your days at work.

Sometimes we know we need a change in employment or career, yet haven't chosen to make it. Don't be surprised if the Universe intervenes and you don't get a choice (in the case of being made redundant or retrenched). Although this may cause much stress, as it could take some time to source a new job, it is very likely that your new place of employment will be more suitable for you. Please trust the process and yourself if you find yourself in this particular situation. Apply stress management techniques as required and remain present to prevent the what-ifs of worry. Be where you are and allow others to support you during the transition. Ask for help if necessary. Others will be happy to assist you.

Only you will truly know what the right career is for you, and only you can choose that for yourself. An alternative to full-time employment may be to start your own part-time business, or study part-time if you'd like a change of direction in your work/career. Study will provide you with mental stimulation as well as new knowledge and skills to make that change possible.

As you heal, grow, and find your balance, not only does this extend into your work, career, and financially, but into all areas of your life and the world around you.

Money is an exchange and what goes around comes around. Therefore, if you reluctantly give with a "fear of lack", that will return to you in the form of your *fear*—expressed as a *lack of* abundant incoming funds. My suggestion is to bless the money you give out and ask or pray that it be returned to you, multiplied.

Environment

As you become more balanced you may find yourself more in alignment with (and even effected by) the environment around you. Geographical location, seasons, and moon cycles all affect our personal energy. This may become more obvious to you over time and with further personal growth.

* * * * * * * *

Allow what is going on around you to be your mirroring guide. Due to the fact that you know your personal energy so well now, you'll begin to become even more aware of how things outside yourself affect you personally. If you sense a disturbance in your being, *stop*! and become fully aware in the present moment.

Where are you?

Who are you with?

What are you doing?

What or who were you just thinking about?

How we respond to our outer world generally reflects the state of our inner world. Be aware when encountering negative or challenging situations. If we think, feel or react negatively, we must determine what it is within ourselves that is being mirrored by the outside world—be it another person, situation or event.

How are you feeling within yourself?

Is your energy high and strong, or low and weak?

What is really at the core of your dis-ease or turbulent energy?

Is there something you need to let go of, or obtain?

What is required to maintain your "pure balance"?

Do you need to take some time-out for self and recharge so you can deal with what is going on around you?

Love yourself enough to give yourself whatever you need, in each precious moment of your life.

Conscious awareness is key...

Be your own private investigator, intuitive seer and guru

in each and every moment...

Instigate healing, growth and empowerment techniques as required

to shift any mis-alignment of energy on

every level of your being—mind, body, heart, and spirit...

Bring yourself back to your personal <u>pure balance point</u>,

again, and again, and again!

AFTERWORD

Wow! It's now six years since I was first guided to write my book, and what a journey this experience has been. My personal self-discovery, healing, growth, and empowerment during this time, continues to astound me. With complete dedication, unwavering faith, hundreds of hours, mountains of energy and love, and basically my entire being expressed through the pages, the dream is now reality—a published product! This fills me with a deep sense of gratitude, fulfilment, and love for all.

Throughout the writing of this book I have continued to nurture myself and expand even further, on all levels—mind, body, heart, and spirit. I have become an enhanced person, wife, mum, and professional for it. As with all earthlings, I continue to learn and grow. Of course life still throws challenges (some of them major) my way, yet today I handle them with more ease and grace. Remaining aware, present in the *now,* and focussing on finding solutions, I trust in and follow my intuition in each moment. Of course I also continuously return to my own point of pure balance.

Over the past couple of years I have observed a dramatic and truly awesome shift in the world and its people. There are many beautiful, balanced souls leading a health and wellbeing revolution. We are so much more than our minds and bodies, and people are now valuing themselves and their health, climbing aboard the wellness train. To give you some examples, complementary and energetic therapies are more widely available, people are beginning to hear about and enjoy healthful foods (like green smoothies), and we are acknowledging and listening to the messages of our emotions. Boys are allowed (and encouraged) to cry, spirituality is now not so "woo woo", and self-care isn't seen as selfish anymore. I am so proud to be a part of it and hope that after reading this book (if you haven't already), you'll join in the transformation too.

As an expression of myself and the messages I wish to portray, I hope you have found *Pure Balance* as it was intended—a useful companion and resource, to support and guide you along your path in life. May you continue with courage and confidence, be all that you were born to be and live life to your fullest capacity! Ultimately the choice is yours. I wish you well and all the best...

In love, light and truth,
Clare x

REFERENCES

There have been a number and variety of sources that have informed my journey. Some are mentioned throughout the book, and others can be found in *Chapter 7—A Little More Help*.

- Hay, Louise L. *Heal Your Body*. Hay House, Inc; 1982.

- Lipton, Bruce H. Ph.D. *The Biology of Belief*. Hay House, Inc; 2005.

- McGuire, Michelle and Beerman, Kathy A. *Nutritional Sciences, from Fundamentals to Food. 3rd Edition* . Yolanda Cossio; 2011.

- Totora and Grabowski. *Principles of Anatomy and Physiology. 9th Edition*. John Wiley and Sons, Inc; 2000.

- Fuhrman, Joel. *Eat to Live*. 2003. Little, Brown and Company; 2003

- www.drfuhrman.com

- www.diseaseproof.com

ABOUT THE AUTHOR

CLARE EVANS

Clare grew up in rural Western Australia and in 2007 faced a major turning point, when she was diagnosed with cancer. At the age of thirty Clare found herself reviewing everything she'd come to know about herself, her life, and the world around her.

As well as accepting the help of modern medicine through chemotherapy, she embarked on an intense journey of self-discovery, healing, and growth. Clare was inspired more than ever to read many self-help books as well as medical literature. She changed many things in her life, both within and without, including a shift in career—from administration to "follow her destiny" in a grounded and balanced way.

In 2011, as part of her healing journey, Clare relocated to New South Wales with her husband and daughters.

After five years in remission Clare was officially cured in 2013. Feeling that she is experiencing her best version of optimal health and wellbeing, Clare wishes to share what she's learnt with others through this book.

CLARE EVANS

A passionate health and wellbeing advocate, Clare's qualifications are in reflexology, holistic counselling, and nutritional education training. She confidently empathises with and assists others amid the knowledge and skills she's gained from study, as well as personally—through many of her own life's lessons and experiences. With over five and half years of experience working with clients one-to-one, Clare's focus is now on speaking and writing for larger audiences.

Her dream is that many people from all over the world begin to heal, grow, and become self-empowered in love—to live happy, healthy, and balanced lives!

Connect with Clare online;

clareevans.com.au